THE ESSENTIAL
MARATHONER

Also by John Hanc

The Essential Runner:
A Concise Guide to the Basics for All Runners

THE
ESSENTIAL

MARATHONER

A Concise Guide to

the Race of Your Life

JOHN HANC

THE LYONS PRESS

Printed in the United States of America

Design by Howard P. Johnson

Illustrations by Mitchell Heinze

10 9 8 7 6 5 4 3

Library of Congress Cataloging-in-Publication Data

Hanc, John.
    The essential marathoner : a concise guide to the race of your life /
John Hanc.
        p.   cm.
    Includes bibliographical references and index.
    ISBN 1-55821-407-0
    1. Marathon running.   2. Marathon running—Training.   I. Title.
GV1065.H26   1996
796.42'5—dc20   96-3440
                                                    CIP

This book is not intended to be a substitute for medical advice. Anyone beginning a running program should receive clearance from their doctor, especially those who are over 45 years old, have a family history of coronary artery disease, or have any of the other risk factors commonly associated with coronary artery disease, such as high blood pressure, high cholesterol levels, diabetes, obesity or cigarette smoking.

C O N T E N T S

Acknowledgments

Many people provided valuable assistance in the planning and writing of this book. First and foremost, I thank Jeff Galloway—the coach, author, and former Olympian whose successful program for first-time marathoners forms the basis of this book and who generously allowed me to use it as such. Very special thanks are also due to the great and gracious Grete Waitz and to Ellie Krieger, M.S., R.D., for her important contributions to our chapter on nutrition. I thank also author Gloria Averbuch, *Runner's World* executive editor Amby Burfoot, and Dr. Edward Fryman, medical director of the Long Island Marathon. I'm happy to call them my friends and thankful for their generous input on this project.

Also, thanks go to Peter Burford and my editor Lilly Golden; to Marie Patrick, Mike Hoy, and the other folks at the City of Los Angeles Marathon for allowing me to be part of a great show; to Jack Fleming of the Boston Athletic Association; and to colleague Gordon Bakoulis, counselor Doug Hynes, confidante Lee Schreiber, and constant supporter Stan Kramberg.

Portions of this book originally appeared in *Women's Sports & Fitness*, *New York Running News*, *Runner's World*, and in my weekly running and fitness columns in the New York and Long Island editions of *Newsday*. My editors at these publications deserve recognition, especially Lisa Peters O'Brien, Raleigh Mayer, Don Mogelefsky, Mark Will-Weber, Cristina Negron, Jill Agostino, and Tony Castineiras.

To my wife, Donna, thanks for the expert (and reasonably priced) clerical and production assistance. To all the runners, coaches, and sports-medicine professionals cited in this book, thanks for sharing your anecdotes, your research, your experiences.

Finally, to you . . . the aspiring or novice marathoner. It's a long road, but worth every step. Good luck!

INTRODUCTION

Back in 1978, not many could have imagined me running a marathon, least of all me. It was my husband Jack's idea, a way to get a trip to the United States, he reasoned. Despite being a world-class track runner, I had run no further than twelve miles—nor had I ever run a road race—when I toed the starting line of my first marathon in New York.

But after all, what did anyone really know about the marathon back then? There was a dearth of training advice and programs—and virtually a total absence of information on subjects like shoes and clothing, nutrition, stretching, or cross-training. In fact, one of my most enduring memories on my first trip through the streets in the New York City Marathon is of the simple act of trying to get a drink of water. I was so inexperienced (the idea of fluid replacement had never even crossed my mind) that when I grabbed the cup in an effort to get some desperately needed liquid, it went all over my face and up my nose—everywhere but where it was supposed to. I had, of course, never practiced the act of drinking on the run.

After nine times victoriously breaking the finish line banner in New York and a string of other marathon successes throughout my career (and yes, a few failures too), it's safe to say I have learned about the event by experience. And while experience is understandably the best teacher, I don't advocate going into the marathon without studying and preparing. But sometimes it's not so simple. While the decision to put your mind and body to the 26.2-mile test should never be taken lightly, it often seems it can become enormously complicated. The wealth of books, articles, and—perhaps the biggest source of information—"friendly advice" all can lead to a lot confusion. But despite all of these resources, I have met literally thousands of marathoners and would-be marathoners in my career—at races and clinics—who still have the same basic, unanswered questions.

I have faced many challenges running marathons—some just part of the game, others perhaps avoidable with a bit of education. And though I clearly "spoke the language" of serious running before undertaking a marathon career, how I wish I could have learned more about the marathon before attempting my first 26.2-mile effort. These days, any marathoner can learn the guidelines. A good book, grounded in the basics, is an excellent start.

The Essential Marathoner is just that guide, filled with practical, basic advice and comprehensive enough for a perfect overview of marathoning.

I'd like to show you how reading this book can help you. Consider my first experience again. After being spurred on by the voluminous crowds along First Avenue in New York, by mile 16 I had really picked up the pace. Now, the concept of "hitting the wall" had of course never occurred to me, since the only walls I knew of were in buildings. But clearly I was running into some walls of my own. By 21 miles, I began looking for trees around every corner I turned. I knew that trees meant a park and that the finish of the race was in Central Park. But so unprepared was I that when I asked another runner how much distance we had to go and he answered five miles, my brain couldn't even compute it to my familiar kilometers. I basically had no idea how much further I had to run.

I won the race that day, setting a world record in the process, but initially after I crossed the line I threw my shoes down on the ground and swore to my husband, "Never again!" Now, if I had read chapter 2 of this book, "Ready to Run a Marathon?", I would have understood in advance what my body and my mind would go through. If I had had chapter 3 to read, "Training to Go the Distance," I could have practiced first with a few long runs. And if I had read chapter 7 about food and fuel during the marathon, I wouldn't have merely splashed water all over myself.

With this book, you can begin your marathon odyssey with the education I didn't have. Thanks to author John Hanc, himself a veteran of eight marathons and with a decade of experience writing on the subject of running and fitness, you have a guide to get you fit and ready to reach the starting line and to prepare you for your 26.2-mile journey. I have told you about my biggest learning experience, my first marathon. What I have not yet mentioned is the wonderful opportunities the marathon has given me: a new career, my New York victories, a world championship gold medal and an Olympic silver medal, world records, and endless other benefits. But mostly, the marathon has given me something everyone can have: a wonderful, endless challenge and enormous personal satisfaction. The marathon is a journey that I have treasured each time I have undertaken it. And I am confident that with this book, it is a journey that you will embark upon with the confidence to know you are as informed and inspired as possible.

—Grete Waitz
Spring 1996

THE MARATHON
MYSTIQUE

1

In 1992, forty-eight-year old Rae Baymiller crossed the finish line of the Twin Cities Marathon, her first. She hasn't been the same since. "I got goose bumps," recalls Baymiller. "I felt that if I could do this, I could do anything."

The marathon will do that to you. There's a mystique about running 26.2 miles . . . as if it's some exotic journey that only a few can take. "If you want to run, run a mile," said Emil Zatopek, the great Czech Olympian of the 1950s. "If you want to experience another life, run a marathon."

Talk like that scares the bejesus out of many beginners. It shouldn't. The truth is, you don't have to be a Tibetan monk or Superman to survive a marathon. Any reasonably healthy individual can do it, provided that they train properly and have the motivation to do it. Proper training and preparation are what this book is about. But motivation has to come from within, especially for someone contemplating their own marathon journey. Here are a few examples of people who have successfully made that journey and what it's meant for them.

"Running the marathon gave me an inner strength that changed my life," says Henley Gibble, executive director of the Road Runners Club of America, who ran her first 26.2-miler back in 1976. "I think that's what happens to a lot of women who complete a marathon. Whether it's fast or slow, whether you walk some of it or not, just finishing can have a profound affect on your confidence and self-esteem."

After thirteen years of running for public office, Douglas Hynes decided to run the New York City Marathon. A three-term councilman for the Town of Oyster Bay on suburban Long Island, Hynes voted no to a re-election bid in 1993. Instead of the campaign trail, he decided to hit the trails of a nearby state park, logging the miles in preparation for the marathon. "It gave me a natural outlet for my competitive spirit," said Hynes. "The same organization, the same determination that politics requires are all required in running." On Marathon Sunday in the Big Apple, Hynes went the distance. "I've never had an experience like this," he said afterward. "And I'll never forget it."

I resolved to run my first marathon in 1985, about a month after my first wife and I separated. It just seemed like the right time to channel all that energy into something else, something different. I was glad I did. The months of training were therapeutic: they helped me focus and concentrate. Afterward, I felt emotionally and physically better than ever.

While I ran to help distance myself from a broken relationship, I've met others who have used running as a way to share time, to work together toward a mutual goal. I met Carl and Nancy Weiner after they finished the 1990 New York City Marathon—their first. They ran together, finishing in 5 hours, 45 minutes, and their reactions were typical of so many people: "Overwhelming!" said Carl, a physician. "An incredible experience! It was like going around the world in a day." Weiner's wife was slightly less exuberant in her praise—she simply compared it to childbirth.

No one can deny that running the marathon will take its toll on you. There will probably be moments during the training and the race when you'll wonder why you're doing it. That's the time to think back to what you're reading here and to remember this simple truth: if doing a marathon were easy, no one would make such a big deal about it.

For most of us, the race itself is the culmination of a larger and more gradual change in lifestyle: it's the ultimate test of our fitness. Few people go directly from the couch to the starting line of a marathon, but with a little determination, almost anybody can get there sooner or later. At age sixty-two, Mavis Lindgren of Orleans, California, could barely walk around the block. At age seventy, she ran her first marathon. Now in her eighties, she holds a number of world age-group records—and she's still running strong. "I want to inspire people to reach their fullest potential," said Lindgren, in a biography of her called *Grandma Wears Running Shoes*. "I want to tell them to dream big dreams—and make them come true."

In the realm of participatory sports, there are few bigger

dreams than completing a marathon, and arguably no bigger star than Oprah Winfrey has ever run one. When she did the Marine Corps Marathon in Washington, D.C., in November 1994, it was headline news all over the country. Viewers had followed her training. Reporters and photographers ran along with her to see if she would make it. She did. In an interview in *Fitness* magazine, she said that finishing the race was an intense and deeply personal moment. "I'm starting to cry," Oprah told writer Nancy Stedman, recalling her emotions near the end. "I'm remembering all those years I struggled with my weight, those times when I saw my reflection in a store window and didn't know who that fat person was, years when it was a big accomplishment for me to exercise at two dots [levels] on the StairMaster. And now I'm finishing a 26.2-mile race. Damn! This is better than winning an Emmy!"

Most of us will never be able to make that comparison, but everyone who finishes a marathon will know what it feels like to be a celebrity—at least for a day. You're cheered by spectators, volunteers, and race officials. You're a hero to those around you. "You're probably not going to win the race, but you will be a winner with your family and friends," says Stan Kramberg, a Bellmore, New York, insurance agent who is so proud of his multiple New York City Marathon completions that he has a vanity license plate reading "RANY5X."

Why all the fuss? "Because," says Stan, "when you've done a marathon, you've done something a lot of people wish they could do."

I was reminded of that fact during the writing of this book. In March 1995 I ran the City of Los Angeles Marathon, my eighth career marathon—and the first one in nearly three years. That night, I entered a trendy West Hollywood restaurant wearing a race T-shirt and my finisher's medal. A tableful of diners stopped eating, rose in unison, and gave me a standing ovation. "You did the whole thing?" one man at the head of the table asked incredulously, as if there weren't fifteen thousand other runners who had accomplished the same thing that morning. "That's terrific! That is just fantastic."

And believe me, despite all the effort, it was fantastic. It will be for you, too.

THE MARATHON: A BRIEF HISTORY

Like baseball, Santa Claus, and the world's major religions, the origins of the marathon are shrouded in myth.

It goes something like this: In 490 B.C., a Greek messenger named Pheidippides ran twenty-four miles from the plains of Marathon to Athens with news of a great victory over the Persians. "Rejoice!" he said. "We conquer." Then he promptly fell dead.

It's a great story, but it probably never happened. The Battle of Marathon most certainly did: it was a major upset as ancient battles go, with the outnumbered Athenian army killing thousands of invading Persians and forcing the rest to flee to their ships. All of this was recorded by the historian Herodotus. But—as researched by Sandy Treadwell, author of the 1987 book *The World of Marathons*—Herodotus never mentions this extended victory lap in his telling of the battle saga. What good historian would miss a story like that? According to Treadwell, Herodotus did mention Pheidippides in another context: he was a professional courier chosen by the Athenians to deliver a message to Sparta asking for help against the invading Persians. Although the Spartans turned down his request—they were in the middle of a holiday feast—Pheidippides made the round-trip run of 150 miles in forty-eight hours, making him perhaps the world's first *ultra*marathoner. Yet he goes down in history as the father of the 26.2-mile race—two miles longer than the run he didn't actually do. Still, the legend probably has much to do with the idea that running a marathon—*any* marathon—is a suicide mission.

This view, still actually believed by some people, seemed validated by what happened in the first years of the modern Olympics. When Pierre de Coubertin revived the Games in 1896, he included the 24-mile run at the behest of one of his colleagues, a Sorbonne scholar named Michel Breal, who remembered the legend of Pheidippides and thought it would be appropriate to commemorate him by including a long run as part of the competition. (In the ancient Olympics, the longest running event was 4,800 meters, a little under three miles.)

Starting by the warrior tomb of the Battle of Marathon, twenty-five runners—most of them Greek—took off on the first modern marathon on April 10, 1896. It was ugly. Several runners collapsed, and one, Australian Edwin Flack, was so out of it that he reportedly punched a spectator who tried to help him after he fell. But in the end, a twenty-four-year-old itinerant goat-herder and mail-carrier named Spiridon Loues was victorious—and all of Greece rejoiced.

In attendance that day in Athens was Tom Burke, a gold

medal sprinter who competed for the Boston Athletic Association. Burke was so inspired by the Olympic marathon that he decided to stage the first great American marathon. The following year, 1897, eighteen men set out from Hopkinton, Massachusetts, for the first running of the Boston Marathon. John J. McDermott of New York was the winner in a time of 2 hours, 55 minutes —10 seconds faster than Loues and 48 minutes slower than Cosma Ndeti's course-record time of 2:07:15 in 1994.

The 1908 London Olympic marathon was among the most important in the event's history: it established the modern marathon distance. To allow the English royal family to view the race, the course was extended so that it reached the private lawns of Windsor Castle—total: 26.2 miles. Despite the occasional race director who likes to hype his five-mile run by calling it a "marathon," 26.2 miles remains the standard distance. (Yes, to answer a commonly asked question, *all* marathons are 26.2 miles.)

The perception of marathon running as athletic insanity was reinforced by the 1908 London Olympic marathon: on that hot summer day, the exhausted twenty-two-year-old leader, Dorando Pietri, wobbled and weaved his way toward the finish line at London Stadium. The old footage makes it seem almost comical. As he enters the stadium, he looks like an extra from a Charlie Chaplin movie who has been conked on the head. But heat exhaustion is no joke; and Pietri's misery was compounded when an official helped steady the diminutive Italian as he crossed the line. A debate arose, Pietri was disqualified, and the victory went to Johnny Hayes—the last American marathon winner in the Olympics for sixty-four years.

Hayes's victory ushered in a mini–running boom in the

United States. Long-distance "pedestrian" events—running and walking—had been popular here throughout much of the nineteenth century. Fans had packed the old Madison Square Garden in New York City and other major venues to watch grueling, six-day "go-as-you-please" indoor races, usually wagering on the winners like they were at a horse race. The momentum of Hayes's victory led to a resurgence in interest in distance running in the 1910s and 1920s, as evidenced by such events as the Bunion Derby transcontinental races, a series of cross-country foot races.

Still, spectators far outnumbered participants. The average American didn't run distances and didn't see any reason why anyone else would want to. As the country settled into its sedentary post-war affluence, runners seemed out of step with the rest of the society. "We were the outcasts," recalled Kurt Steiner, a co-founder of the New York Road Runners Club and an Olympic racewalker and marathoner in the 1950s. "People looked at us like were a bunch of guys running in our underwear."

That began to change in the late 1960s. A number of factors contributed to the rise of the health and fitness boom in this country. One of them was Dr. Kenneth Cooper's bestselling book *Aerobics*, published in 1968, which added a new word to the language and put a new spring in the step of many hitherto sedentary Americans. Four years later, Frank Shorter's victory in the 1972 Olympic marathon in Munich added new glamour and visibility to the event. Shorter was a Yale-educated, articulate, and well-prepared athlete who looked nothing like Dorando Pietri at the end of the race, prompting many middle- and upper-class Americans to hit the roads, beginning an era that would later be called the "Running Boom" of the 1970s.

At around the same time, pioneering women marathoners—such as Kathrine Switzer and Nina Kuscsik—were challenging rules that prohibited women from running long-distance races. In 1967, Switzer managed to enter the Boston Marathon—which still barred women entrants—by filling out her application as "K. Switzer." In an episode captured in a famous series of photographs, Boston Marathon race director Jock Semple tried to forcibly drag Switzer off the course when he discovered what she had done. Her hammer-thrower boyfriend stopped him, and she managed to finish the race, albeit unofficially. But the impact of the women's movement in every aspect of American society was being felt on the roads, as well. By the time of the 1972 New York City Marathon, the American Athletic Union finally agreed to sanction women in marathons. But officials still demanded a separate start, ten minutes prior to the men. Led by Kuscsik, the women participants in the women's race staged a "sit-in" at the starting line to protest. Kuscsik went on to win the women's race, and the AAU—which was subsequently sued for discrimination—lost the battle. The following year in New York, men and women started together.

Although the sit-in was a *cause célèbre*, the marathon in the nation's largest city was still a small event. The first New York City Marathon, held in September 1970 in Central Park, attracted a total of 127 starters—only 55 of whom finished. That changed in 1976, when the New York Road Runners Club, led by visionary president Fred Lebow, managed to persuade city officials to allow him to plan a race—ostensibly as part of the nation's bicentennial celebration—through all five boroughs of the city, from a breathtaking start on the Staten Island side of the Verrazano Bridge, through Brooklyn, Queens, the East Side of Manhattan, a short hop into the Bronx, and back into Manhattan, for a Central Park finish. On October 24, 1976, the first five-borough New York City Marathon was held—and it was probably on that date that modern marathoning for the masses was born. Not surprisingly, the number of participants in New York grew from 534 in 1975 (when the race was still five loops of the park) to 2,090 in 1976. The winner in '76 was the other great marathon hero of the '70s—Bill Rodgers, who went on to win both New York and Boston four times.

Rodgers was a Massachusetts schoolteacher whose easygoing nature and boyish appearance gave lots of American men the idea that if he could do it, so could they. And they could—despite the fact that few of them had Rodgers' talent. Still, inspired by Shorter, Rodgers, and Jim Fixx's 1977 best-seller, *The Complete Book of Running*, more and more ordinary folks began to take on the extraordinary challenge of the marathon. The numbers of runners and races began to skyrocket: in New York alone, the number of participants grew to 14,000 by 1980—and just as important, the vast majority of those who started finished.

Another American, Alberto Salazar, won New York three times in the early 1980s and became yet another national marathon star. But the next great leap forward for the event occurred in 1984, when Joan Benoit (now Joan Samuelson) won the first women's Olympic marathon in Los Angeles and a runner of relatively advanced age, thirty-seven-year-old Carlos Lopes of Portugal, won the men's gold. Benoit, one of the most tenacious runners in marathon history, became an overnight (and somewhat reluctant) celebrity in the United States, further adding to the marathon luster and providing a new athletic role model for women. Meanwhile, Grete Waitz of Norway was en route to winning nine New York City marathons and earning a place—along with her friend and patron, the goateed Lebow—as one of the most popular and recognizable sports figures in New York in the 1980s.

Over the last ten years, there have been many great marathoners, but few of them American or known to the average American. Italians and, more recently, African and Mexican runners have dominated the event. It's a shame that so few people in this country recognize the achievements of a runner like Ndeti, the great Kenyan who won Boston three years in a row. Still, almost everybody seems to appreciate and respect any individual who can finish a marathon, no matter how long it takes them—one reason perhaps that the numbers of marathon participants have continued to grow through the 1990s.

The number of races themselves—which have long since become established and, in many cases, profitable events—has shot up, too. The last couple of years have marked a succession of anniversaries among the country's largest marathons. In 1995, Los Angeles celebrated its tenth anniversary, and the Marine Corps Marathon in Washington, D.C., its twentieth. Nineteen ninety-six marks the twentieth anniversary of the five-borough New York City Marathon, the one hundredth running of the granddaddy of American marathons, Boston, not to mention the Olympic marathon in Atlanta. In all of these races, marathoners of all levels— from the first-rate to the first-timers—will follow again in legendary footsteps.

2

READY TO RUN
A MARATHON?

The impossible dream. For many people, that kind of sums up the idea of trying to cover 26.2 miles on two feet. It seems overwhelming. Superhuman. Mind-and-body-boggling.

As is typical of most major marathons, about one-third of the 27,500 runners who lined up at the start of the 25th New York City Marathon on November 6, 1994, were first-timers. It's safe to say that they were all just like you, at one point . . . just as intimidated by the idea of a marathon, just as uncertain as to whether they could go the distance.

They did, and you can, too—if you're willing to pay the price.

"The marathon is demanding physically, demanding emotionally, and demanding on your social structures," says Dr. Edward Fryman, medical director of the Long Island Marathon. "It takes a lot of concentration and planning."

Many marathoners say that the four to six months of necessary training for the race is like having a part-time job, particularly on the weekends, when most runners do the long training runs that can keep them on the road for up to four hours. (We'll get to those in the next couple of chapters.)

That's a long time and a lot of pounding on the body. So, is this fitness or madness? "I think it borders on both," says Dr. Michael Kelly, director of the Insall-Scott-Kelly Institute for Orthopedics and Sports Medicine at Beth Israel Hospital in Manhattan. "It really beats up the skeletal system. But it can be done safely. I would not discourage someone from trying to run a marathon. I would just emphasize the seriousness of it."

Certainly, a marathon puts serious stress on the body. Dr. Mark Caselli of the New York College of Podiatric Medicine estimates that during a 26-mile run the feet strike the ground about 35,000 times—at a force three to four times greater than body weight. For a 160-pound man, that's as much a 640 pounds of pressure generated through the foot every time it hits the ground.

Proper shoes and running form can help minimize the impact, but you also need a level of aerobic conditioning that will enable you to keep moving for the three, four, or five hours it takes the average beginner to cover 26.2 miles. That level of fitness is built up slowly, by adding one or two miles to long runs, every other week, for several months.

Progression at such a snail's pace doesn't sit well with

some would-be runners, who approach the race fueled by unrealistic goals and a gross underestimation of what's involved. Bob Glover, coach of the New York Road Runners Club, likes to tell about a woman who came to him a few weeks before the New York City Marathon and announced she was ready, because she was in good cardiovascular condition from stationary biking. Glover agreed. "You're well on your way," he told the woman, "to running *next* year's marathon."

Fryman sees a lot of patients who are so excited after watching the marathon on TV that they want to go directly from the living room couch to the starting line. "I'm a little leery about that," he says, "especially if they've just started running." Kelly agrees. "I think that anyone who wakes up one morning and decides to do a marathon should start by getting a physical to make sure everything's working okay," he says. And like most experts, he believes anyone considering a marathon should already have been running regularly—three or four times a week, 3 to 5 miles per session—for close to a year.

In other words, become a runner first, and then a marathoner.

Sounds like a long time and a lot of work? It is, but as you heard from a range of people in chapter 1, the rewards are worth it. Remember also that 80 percent of those who enter a marathon finish it. And that's a conservative figure, because it includes people who may have registered the race but never ended up running. In the larger marathons, the finishing percentages are even higher: nearly 95 percent of those runners who started the 1994 New York Marathon finished, a statistic that's been fairly consistent in that race over the past decade.

Nationwide, interest in the marathon continues to grow—a decade after the so-called Running Boom leveled off in this country. According to the USA Track & Field Road Running Information Center in Santa Barbara, California, there were about 324,500 marathon finishers in 1994, an 8 percent increase over the previous year. "It's pretty astounding," says Ryan Lamppa, a researcher at the center. "It's definitely a growth race. The race directors are doing a good job marketing their events. And there's no question about the marathon mystique: it's kind of a badge of honor. You tell people 'I've done a 10K,' no big deal. You say 'I've done a marathon,' their ears perk up."

WHO CAN RUN THE MARATHON?

In a word, anyone. That is, any healthy individual willing to put in the time and effort. As we've said, you should already have an established running base before you begin marathon training. That doesn't mean that you have to be a good runner or a competitive runner, it just means that you've already given your body a chance to adapt to the stresses of running and that your body has reaped some of those benefits of the activity.

When *shouldn't* you run a marathon? The most obvious answer is when you're sick. But even then, it depends on the individual and the illness. In 1992, I was a part of a group who accompanied New York Marathon director Fred Lebow through his emotional and inspiring completion of the race he co-founded in 1970. Two years earlier, Lebow had been diagnosed with brain cancer. This is not to say that anyone with a serious illness should consider running a marathon. That's a question for the doctors—and their answers will probably be, sensibly, "not now." When Lebow ran his last, he was already a veteran of sixty-eight marathons. He knew what he had to do to get ready. But it just goes to show that the marathon field is a wide-open one.

Beginners, I think, should look at other factors while making the decision to run. What's going on in your life right now? Are you about to change a job, start a family, buy a house, make a major move of some sort? If so, it might be wise to wait a few months or a year before taking on the marathon challenge. Not because you have to live like a monk to train for a marathon, but simply because it takes time and energy—over and above the time and energy you already put into your job, your family, and so forth. If additional major stresses or changes are going on in your life, you're probably not going to have the energy it takes to prepare properly, and to enjoy . . . yes, *enjoy* . . . the training.

Aside from those caveats, I'll say it again: any healthy individual can run a marathon provided that they are willing to put in the time and preparation necessary to train properly.

Consider the 18,796 entrants to the 1994 Los Angeles Marathon (see Appendix II). There were high school hotshots in their teens and grandmothers in their eighties; there were fat runners, short runners, fast runners, slow runners. There were men and women of every race and background and occupation. There were bartenders and beauticians, college professors and clergymen, Hollywood moguls and hash-house cooks. This is one of the wonderful things about marathoning today: it's a very democratic sport. You don't need to stand seven feet tall or weigh 300 pounds. You don't need to have the eyes of a .300 hitter or the quickness of a prize fighter. You don't even need to be fast! What you do need is will: the will to abide by a training program. The will to get up a couple of hours earlier on Saturday or Sunday morning to get your long run in. The will to structure your life a bit more over the next few months: to get more sleep, drink more fluids, eat more carefully. Some would argue that this is what we should be doing all the time, which is one of the nice things about training for a marathon.

I've heard many people say it and I agree: you never feel fitter than when you're in marathon shape.

Conversely, many people will tell you that they've never looked worse; never been as gaunt, never been as tired, never been as prone to colds and other minor ailments. And there is medical research to show that the immune system can be depressed after a marathon. But if you train, eat, and rest sufficiently and properly, if you give yourself enough time to build up to the marathon and to recover from it, you shouldn't have a problem.

Believe me, I know. I broke most of the rules while preparing for my first marathon: I packed four months of training into two and a half. I did long runs every week. I never took a day off and hardly ever bothered to stretch. What happened? I got a cold two weeks before the race, and although I finished and was very proud, I had a miserable time during the race.

I learned from those mistakes; and I'm happy to report that I felt a lot better before, during, and after my next seven marathons. That's one of the reasons I'm writing this book: to help you avoid some of the mistakes that so many first-timers make. But don't make the mistake of thinking that you can't do it just because you don't think you're very athletic, or built for it, or that you're not fast. None of that matters. The goal of every beginner should be to finish a marathon—nothing more. What matters is your will, your heart. The kind of heart demonstrated by some of the remarkable people who run marathons every year. Of all the stories I've heard, none is more inspiring than the amazing saga of Elaine Kirchen. In the ten years I've been writing about this sport, it is the story that has elicited the biggest reaction from readers. And with good reason.

On December 15, 1989, Kirchen stepped off a Manhattan curb and was hit by a limousine. Pinned under the driveshaft, she had to be freed by a crane. She had broken fifteen ribs and her pelvis, collarbone, and breastbone. Both lungs were punctured, and one collapsed. She was on life support for a week, in the intensive-care unit for two weeks and completely immobilized for five weeks.

When Kirchen emerged from the hospital that February, she could barely walk. When she was fit enough to start running, she couldn't go further than a half mile. "I was in constant oxygen debt because of the damage to my lungs," she said. "I had to stop and catch my breath every few steps." She progressed from long painful walks in February to a run of two-thirds of a mile in March to marathon training by the summer. And then, on November 4, 1990, less than a year after the accident, Kirchen ran the New York City Marathon.

When one of her doctors heard this, Kirchen recalled, "He said I had returned from the dead."

Kirchen is alive and well and running today. Granted,

she was an exceptionally talented runner to begin with—
she was the top masters (over 40) finisher at the 1988
Olympic Trials Marathon, where her time was 2 hours, 46
minutes. Her 1990 New York time was an hour slower. But,
she said with a laugh, "Considering that ten months before
I couldn't walk across the room, it's all right."

All right? It's amazing. And, as her coach Tracy Sundlun
points out, Kirchen's courage and determination offer a lesson for all of us. "Her greatest strength was her mind," said
Sundlun. "Her mind allowed her to take those first steps,
her mind allowed her to come back as fast as she did. The
body is generally capable of much more than the mind
realizes."

When the time comes—as it inevitably will during your
training—that you wonder if you can go the distance, think
of Elaine Kirchen, who "returned from the dead" to run a
marathon. You'll realize that if you put your mind to it, anything is possible. Even a marathon.

3

Training to Go
the Distance

"**You have no chance of** winning. No one will give you a medal. You are not a contender for the Mercedes. But you are going to run this race, a staggering long distance, and you will pay for it. The payments will start not that first Sunday in March, but months before when your running week gradually expands from 15 miles to 50. Pain will ricochet around your legs and feet, evading your ice packs and stretches; doubts will invade your confidence, eroding your determination. Your feet will sprout blisters, your toenails will turn black with the blood that wells up beneath them; you will wonder sometimes what the point is, but you might as well ask about life. As far as you know, there isn't one."

It sounds like something a French existentialist might have said on a particularly gloomy day. It was actually written by Judith Lewis and appeared as the cover story of the March 9, 1995, issue of *LA Weekly*, the edition that came out the week of the City of Los Angeles Marathon. I picked it up in my hotel, the day before the race—and if I hadn't traveled three thousand miles to run that marathon (and hadn't run seven marathons before and had some confidence in what I was doing), I would have probably packed up my bags, turned around, and headed back to the airport.

The problem with the story of Lewis's training odyssey is that it perpetuates some of the worst myths about marathons and how to train for them: for example, that you have to be crazy to do it, that it's all relentless pain, that it's asking your body to do the impossible.

None of that is true. So why did Lewis seem to have such an awful time of it? Well, in her story, Lewis tells us that during her build-up program, she trained seven days a week. Mistake. With the exception of the talented elite, few distance runners hit the roads seven days a week anymore. And if they do, they don't continue for long: the body—or at least, most bodies—will eventually break down. Certainly, no recreational runner training for his or her first marathon should run seven, six, or even five days a week— and it's doubtful that you should even come within hailing distance of a 50-mile training week.

As far as the pain and all that, well, as we've said earlier, your determination will indeed be tested during your marathon build-up period. And there will be moments of discomfort, maybe even pain, during the training and during the race—but the truth is that you can finish the marathon without sacrificing your body, your sanity, or your toenails. The majority of first-time marathon programs—including the one offered in this book—have eschewed the "no pain, no gain" approach of years ago. Today's watchwords in marathon training are consistency, gradual improvement, and moderation.

And these programs work. They'll get you across the finish line in one piece.

But let's backtrack a little first. People have been trying to figure out the best way to prepare the human body to run 26.2 miles since the marathon distance was first established. Marathon training programs in the first half of the century varied, to say the least: Ellison "Tarzan" Brown, winner of the 1936 Boston Marathon, chopped wood as part of his regimen. Coach Percy Cerutty, who worked with many of the great Australian distance runners of the 1950s and 1960s, had his athletes lift weights, swim, eat raw vegetables, and run up sand dunes until they threw up. In 1914, Boston winner Jimmy Duffy's training program seemed to consist primarily of carousing late into the night. (His first words after crossing the finish line were "Give me a cigarette.")

Most marathoners—and most distance runners in those days—had a track background. They were competitive, talented, and experienced in shorter distances before making the move up to 26.2 miles. But most of these runners and their coaches recognized that you couldn't complete a marathon on a base of quarter-mile repeats. You needed to gradually build up endurance, through regular runs of progressively longer distances. That still holds true today. The running hasn't changed, but the runners have.

"The old question was, 'What do I have to do to win?'"

says Amby Burfoot. "Now the question is, 'What do I have to do to finish?'"

That's a critical difference—and there are few better people in this country to recognize and explain that difference than Burfoot. In 1968, Burfoot, then a college senior at Wesleyan University, won the Boston Marathon. Twenty-five years and about twenty-five marathons later, he returned to Boston, this time as a middle-aged, middle-of-the-pack runner—and the executive editor of *Runner's World* magazine. In his job at the magazine, Burfoot has probably written, edited, abided by, reviewed, and rejected more marathon training programs and articles than anyone in America. As a runner himself—one who has practiced at both the elite and recreational levels—he knows what's it's like to train to go the distance.

"Among the guys I was training with in the 1960s, there was hardly anyone slower than 2 hours, 50 minutes," recalls Burfoot, who was coached by 1957 Boston Marathon winner John J. Kelley. "Today, there are thousands and thousands of runners who do the marathon, and most of them are slower than that. But history has shown that you can get away with fairly little and still do it. I think the key thing is to apply that 'fairly little' consistently over a two- to three-month period. I don't think it's very smart to do very little every Saturday morning and expect to finish the race. But if it's applied consistently over the months, then it can do something. . . . It can get you across the finish line."

Of course, "fairly little" is a decidedly vague term. But I'll tell you this much: it's not 50 miles a week . . . that is, if you're like most first-timers—someone with a life outside of running, with a goal of finishing the race and feeling good about it.

To accomplish that goal, as Burfoot says, you have to be consistent. Just how one properly prepares the mind and body for a 26.2-mile run is a matter of some—but not extreme—debate. There are many well-proven training programs that you can follow, and some of them contradict one another in the fine print. But, especially when you're talking about first-timers, all agree on a few points.

First, you should probably decide which marathon you're going to run before you start training for it, so that you have a specific goal and so you can plan your training schedule to culminate on that day.

There are more than 350 marathons held in the United States annually. They range in size from the Bulldog Marathon in Althus, Oklahoma, which had all of 25 participants last year, to the New York City Marathon, which had more than 25,000. (For a list of some of the largest, see Appendix II.) Marathons vary in other ways, as well, including temperature, terrain, and atmosphere.

"Choose one that has some significance to you," suggests Benji Durden of Boulder, Colorado, a coach and 1980 Olympic marathoner. "Run your hometown race, or go to a city you've always wanted to see." Forty-two-year-old Chris Shihadeh of Portland, Oregon, ran the 1993 New York City Marathon her first time out. "I'd recommend traveling to your first," she says. "It takes away from the drudgery of training to run someplace new and exciting. For me, it became a trip to New York for the weekend—and I got a great tour."

Next, don't choose for your first marathon a race that's being held in two weeks or even two months. Another point most marathon coaches agree on is that good preparation takes time: sixteen weeks at least, if you have been running 3 to 5 miles three or four times per week for a year.

When your selection of a marathon is made, it's time to get started with a training program. Most of the important marathon coaches in America today are pretty consistent in what they see as the fundamental elements of a successful first-time program:

- Long runs
- Proper nutrition
- Rest
- Cross-training

These core principles are practically an outline for this book: we'll look more closely at each of these elements, as they pertain to marathon training, in the pages to come. We'll also incorporate the wisdom of many coaches and experts, but the program that I recommend to beginners is the one developed by Jeff Galloway, a 1972 Olympian. Over the past fifteen years, Galloway, based in Atlanta, Georgia, has coached about five thousand first-time marathoners in his camps and clinics around the country, and he claims a 98 percent success rate, which is one of the best in the business. His conservative 16-week program is based on just *three* days of running a week (plus cross-training) in order to encourage rest and moderation.

Rest and *moderation* are probably the two most overlooked aspects of a marathon training program. The tendency for most beginning marathoners is to get out and work, work, work. And there's plenty of work to be done—but it must be done intelligently, carefully, and gradually. I can tell you firsthand that Galloway's program works. I know, because I broke every one of his principles while training for my first marathon: I started too late; ran too long, too frequently; and didn't get enough rest. I was young and lucky enough to finish my race, but had I been writing about the sport then, my story would have probably sounded a lot more like Judith Lewis's.

The next time around, I did it his way. It was a much better experience, and it gave me the confidence to take my marathoning to the next level—where the idea is not only to finish but to finish within a certain time.

Let's talk about time for a moment. The world record for the fastest marathon currently belongs to Belayneh Densimo of Ethiopia, who finished the 1988 Rotterdam Marathon in a mind-boggling time of 2 hours, 6 minutes, and 50 seconds. The world's best generally do 2:10 or better. The qualifying time for the men's 1996 U.S. Olympic Trials Marathon was 2:20.

Ingrid Kristiansen of Norway holds the women's marathon record: she ran the 1985 London Marathon in a time of 2:21:06. Anything below 2:30 is considered a superb time for a woman marathoner. For American women, the qualifying time to compete in the 1996 Olympic Trials Marathon was 2:50.

Now that you know that, forget about time. "Your goal in your first marathon should be to finish," says Jeff Galloway. "Don't worry about how fast."

He's right. The marathon, as Grete Waitz often says, is a learning process: every time you run one, you learn more about the event and about yourself. You may choose to never again run a marathon after your first one; you may do one a year for the rest of your life. Either way, the first thing you have to do as a novice marathoner is teach your body and your mind to go the distance; it doesn't matter how fast. The long runs you'll do as part of your training program will give you the endurance and strength to finish 26.2 miles. Every coach will tell you that. But Amby Burfoot believes that the mental part of the training shouldn't be overlooked. "At some level, running a marathon is easy," he says. "It's getting yourself prepared, that's where all the effort is. And a large part of that effort is mental."

TRAINING THE MIND FOR THE MARATHON

Recently, a new health club opened in Manhattan. Called The Mind Gym, it is designed to help train the mind in the way regular gyms help people train the body. The founders, a motivational expert and an attorney, had a sense of humor about it: instead of exercise mats or Steps, the gym's main studio is set up with dozens of the leather recliners typically associated with a psychiatrist's office.

Still, their purpose is a serious one. In order to succeed in reaching your goals—whether the goal is to lose weight or quit smoking—you need to train the mind as well as the body. Can you train yourself mentally to finish a marathon? Obviously, the best attitude in the world won't compensate for the necessary physical training. Ideally, you'll have the proper balance of both. But the mental aspect is a crucial and often overlooked aspect of training. It is an important part of any program, especially because marathon horror stories like Lewis's have turned the marathon into an athletic Everest for the average person.

In an article entitled "Think Like a Champion" in the August 1994 issue of *Runner's World*, Jerry Lynch, Ph.D., a sports psychologist from Santa Cruz, California, listed what he believes are the keys to mental success. Here, in abbreviated form, are six of his mental strategies designed to help you run stronger. For first-time marathoners, who shouldn't be competing against anything but the distance and themselves, some of these are especially appropriate.

THE "I CAN DO" CREDO

We are capable of those things we believe we are capable of. Do you believe you can run a marathon? If you do, then chances are good that you're right. If amputee-athlete Dick Traum of the Achilles Track Club could do the 1994 New York City Marathon on crutches, you can do it on two good legs, aided in no small part by a positive attitude and the belief that you can do it.

LEARNING FROM FAILURE

To succeed, every runner must learn to deal with mistakes and failures. We have all learned everything we know physically—from walking to running a marathon—by trial and error, so there's no reason to become our own worst enemies when we suffer a setback. From time to time, we all fall short of our goals. An accepting attitude helps you perform with greater relaxation, which, as all champions know, is one of the key building blocks of success.

A New Definition of Winning

Too many runners suffocate their enjoyment of running by overemphasizing the importance of fast times. While running, focus on the internal battle: concentrate on overcoming fear, self-doubt, and other limiting beliefs. Forget about external issues, like your time. Such outward concerns will only deplete your energy, create tension, and slow you down.

The Opponent as Friend

When we come together to try to reach our potential, such as in a road race (and particularly a marathon), other participants can only help us. With such a view, you will enter a race more relaxed, focused, and energized. You can't help but perform better as a result of cooperation rather than antagonism.

This is particularly true in marathoning, where a training partner can help you get through long runs. They're not competing with you—they're helping you achieve your goals—as is everyone else around you on race day.

The Power of Simplicity

The true champion recognizes that excellence often flows most smoothly from simplicity, a fact that can get lost in these high-tech days. Don't let gadgets and an overemphasis on schedules get in the way of your enjoyment of the sport. Concentrate instead on the simple act of running.

Moderation and Balance

More isn't better. Moderation is better. Runners who think like champions know when they have done enough. Doing too much, especially in training, is one of the greatest misfortunes a runner can encounter because it can wipe out all your hard-earned conditioning.

THE LONG RUN:
THE SECRET TO
MARATHON SUCCESS

You still want to run a marathon? Well then you should know that the secret to success lies in the *long run*.

"It's the single most important element in any marathon training program," says Gordon Bakoulis of Manhattan, an Olympic Trials marathoner, author, and coach. "You can't fake the fact that your body's going to cover 26.2 miles."

The long run, in the context of marathon training, means a slow training run, starting at whatever distance you're already able to cover, that gradually gets longer until, over a period of weeks, you've built up to nearly 26.2 miles. The long runs teach your body many things: how to deal with fatigue, how to most efficiently burn endurance fuels (carbohydrates and fat), and how to simply keep on your feet and moving for hours at a time.

"The skeletal shock of running a marathon is significant," says Benji Durden. "By doing the long runs, you train your bones to become stronger. The bone density actually increases."

While long runs are invaluable, they are also, well, *long*. As you can see from the week-by-week training program in Appendix I, we're talking about runs of 22 to 24 miles. How to get through them safely and sanely is the focus of this chapter.

To prevent injury and burnout, Galloway adds a modifier to his long-run recipes: take regular walking breaks during each one—a minute of walking for every three to five minutes of running. "Walking breaks decrease the risk of injury," he says. "They force you to keep a conservative pace." Your training speed, according to Galloway, should be at least two minutes per mile slower than your race pace (or the fastest speed you think you can maintain over the distance).

This idea of walking doesn't sit well with some people. The point is to *run* the marathon, right? But Galloway claims that since he started making walking intervals a part of his beginner's program, the injury rate has decreased dramatically. Most of the people that did get injured were those who ignored that advice.

There are other successful coaches who don't force the walking breaks on their first-timers. But they all stress the importance of doing these runs slowly. How slowly? Benji Durden recommends that you go at least two minutes per mile slower than your 10K pace.

The reason I recommend Galloway's program is that it's tailored for first-timers and for those who might not know their 10K pace. It's very simple to follow, and it's extremely conservative. It's a program that anybody—not just hard-bodies—can use to achieve marathon success. Still, as any physician or physiologist will tell you, we are all an experiment of one; that is, we are each unique, and no one rule of thumb can be applied strictly across the board. If you're a young, fit, forty-minute 10K runner doing your first marathon, you may not need to take a one-minute walking break every three minutes during your long runs. But you sure as heck can't go out at a 6:00 pace and hope to survive a 15-miler. What you might try, as a sort of compromise, is a five-minute walking break every thirty minutes. That way, you'll still be giving your body a break, but you won't be constantly looking at your watch, counting off three-minute intervals.

Whatever you do, remember that patience is a virtue, especially in marathon training. Long runs can take a lot out of you. If you try to do them too frequently or increase the distance too rapidly, you'll probably get discouraged or injured. That's why it's best to go long only every other week—to allow the body plenty of time to recover. That's also why the distance of the long run is built up by only 1 to 2 miles at a time, until you're near marathon distance. *How* near is one of the controversies about marathon training: some coaches counsel runners to do more than 26 miles. Others recommend three or four runs of 20 miles each, but no longer. And a few lucky runners have managed to do the marathon having run no further than 12 miles.

I wouldn't look at the 12-milers as role models, however. Most of those who try to run a marathon on a base of a 12- or even 15-mile long run will end up in the race results as a dreaded DNF (that stands for "Did Not Finish").

An example at the other end of the spectrum is overdistance training. Consider Mark Nenow, a former American record holder at 10,000 meters. In 1988, Nenow decided to run his first marathon. "I ran some big-time training for the New York Marathon," he told Gregor Robin of the Santa Barbara *News-Press*. "Big-time" included three 31-mile runs at a six-minute pace. "That aggravated a leg problem that had started to develop earlier in the year. It became chronic," Nenow said. "At the time I didn't know it, but that was the beginning of the end, because I ran New York on the leg and it was a mess."

Nenow retired from competitive running soon afterward. So much for training runs *over* 26 miles.

How about 20 miles? Many programs recommend 20 miles as the longest distance you should do in training. The reasoning is that by going over 20, you increase the risk of injury without appreciably adding to your fitness. Adherents to these programs generally do three or four 20-milers in the weeks prior to the marathon and add the last 10K (or 6.2 miles) on race day. For second- or third-time marathoners, runs no longer than 20 miles are adequate. Running multiple 20-milers make sense, especially if you're training to improve your times: you can focus on going a little faster in training instead of merely farther.

But for first-timers, the idea is not to run for time but to run to finish; and the challenge is almost as much mental as physical. Believe me, a 10K seems like a very long way to go when you've already gone 20 miles. In fact, it's often said that the marathon *begins* at 20 miles. Because that's when the going really gets tough.

For that reason, Galloway recommends building up to 26 miles in your training runs. That way, he maintains, there's no doubt as to whether you're capable of covering the distance. "By running the distance prior to a race," he says, "you're giving your body and mind notice that they will be called upon to go that far."

My preference falls somewhere in the middle—literally. I recommend that you build up to about 22 to 24 miles in your longest training run. Why not 26? Because *that's* the goal. *That's* the challenge. To go the distance in training would make the race almost anticlimactic—and certainly wouldn't help your chances of not getting injured. When you finish your last long run, you want to be confident, but you also want to leave something for race day. It will make crossing that finish line taste even sweeter.

Finally, no matter how far you go in your long runs, you need to build in a decent interval between your last long run and the race: traditionally, two weeks has been recommended, but recent research suggests that three weeks is even better because the body has another week to rest and recuperate. You may get a little antsy, but that's better than feeling worn-out on race day.

We'll leave the last word on long runs to Trevor Smith, who offered some good advice on the topic in *Running & FitNews*, the newsletter of the American Running and Fitness Association. "Do you really need to train beyond 20 miles?" wrote Smith. "While it is not essential, it is mostly a good idea. If you train up to 22 to 24 miles you will have the endurance for your marathon after a three-week recovery taper. Be flexible with your long runs, and remember extra rest not only doesn't hurt, but frequently leads to dramatic improvement."

KEEPING TRACK

It may seem like a fine distinction, but many coaches now recommend that you focus on time, not distance, in your training runs. It helps keep you from becoming a "mileage junkie," someone obsessed with maintaining certain weekly mileage totals.

It's tempting to focus on weekly mileage totals. Most beginners do that instinctively, no matter what a coach or author tells them to do. The challenge here, after all, it seems, is to cover 26.2 miles—not to meet a time goal. In addition, the satisfaction of seeing your improvement, the progressively longer distances you cover in your long runs, will be greater if you count it in miles as opposed to minutes.

But mileage isn't the only thing you should be focused on during your long runs. Running 50 miles over the course of one week has little bearing on whether you will be able to run 26.2 miles on one morning. The long runs are learning experiences—not just for your body and its fuel-burning system but for every aspect of your running. Listen to your body during these runs: how does it feel during certain weather conditions, in warmth, in cool weather, in rain. Can you run better on water or sports drinks, with breakfast or without? Some of these things you should already know as a runner. Still, these marathon training distances are unchartered territory for most of us the first time out. "Use the long run to its fullest," says Stu Mittleman, an exercise physiologist and national champion ultradistance runner (an "ultra" is any race over 31 miles or 50K). "Ask yourself, 'Where do I hurt after the run? What muscles are sore? Do I feel dehydrated? What about my shoes; were they laced too tight?

Did I wear the right socks?' Use it as a form of self-assessment."

And record that data in your training log. If you haven't kept one before, this is the time to begin. The log can simply be a handwritten record in a notebook, or you can get fancy and use the computerized training logs advertised in the back of most of the major running magazines. However you choose to do it, make sure you keep track of your distances or the amount of time you were out there on your feet, the weather, and your feelings—physical and mental— as you build up to the race of your life.

GETTING THROUGH
YOUR LONG RUNS

We've talked about one way to make them more tolerable—walking breaks. Another key is proper hydration. Plan routes that allow you to get water every few miles—from your home, public fountains, or even bottles you stash along the way. Remember, the biggest single risk you face during training runs, as well as during the marathon itself, is dehydration. Drink plenty of water before, during, and after your runs. And if you prefer a sports drink, go right ahead: research has shown that the so-called replacement drinks are most effective in replacing nutrients lost in activities that last ninety minutes or more.

Two of my friends, Doug Hynes and Bill Gilmartin, took some extra steps to make sure they had plenty to drink while preparing for their marathon debut in 1992. They were planning to do the Marine Corps Marathon, held that year at the end of October, so they were already well into their long runs in July and August. To beat the heat, they would get up early, fill several bottles with water, drive out along the course, and stash them every couple of miles. Yes, it was extra effort, it meant getting up an hour earlier, and so forth. But it kept them hydrated and happy through their long runs. The night after the Marine Corps, as we celebrated their first marathon, they recalled those early-morning water-stashing trips; both agreed that they wouldn't have completed their long runs, and therefore their marathon, if it hadn't been for the water laid out along the course.

There is another lesson to learn about long runs from their experience. Hynes and Gilmartin trained together from the start to the finish. That is not uncommon. In fact, some say the best way to get through your long runs is to share the road with a friend or two. "You can't do them alone," says Mike Polansky, a veteran of over forty marathons (he's actually lost count) since 1978 and president of the 1,000-member Plainview–Old Bethpage Road Runners Club on Long Island, New York. "You have to do it with people whose company you enjoy. It makes the miles go. Anybody who can go out and do an 18-miler by themselves is either one hell of a loner or has a lot more mental discipline than I have."

Well, I am neither a loner nor a Zen master, but I did train for one marathon alone, and while the peace and solitude were welcome for part of the way, I have to agree with Polansky. After two hours, you begin to run out of things to think about—except the running—which only makes it tougher. On the other hand, I know several very successful marathon runners who train alone almost all of the time.

Once again, it's an individual choice. You're going to be spending two, three, even four hours on the road. Make that time as pleasant as possible. If that means blessed solitude, fine. If not, seek out the company of a friend or a group of runners. Your local running club probably holds group runs of varying distances and paces on weekends. (If you're not sure of the location of the club nearest you, you can call the Road Runners Club of America in Virginia at (703) 836-0558.)

The New York Road Runners Club stages weekly long runs leading up to the New York City Marathon, and as many as a thousand people show up for some of the scheduled long runs in Central Park. Typically, runners find a couple of like-minded souls whose company they enjoy. Polansky has a friend he argues politics with as the miles roll by. "We never convince each other about any issue," says Polansky. "If we did, we might have to stop running."

Chris Shihadeh trained for her first marathon with four other women and enjoyed their company throughout the race, too. "We stuck together, chatting," she explained. "We were really into the fact that we were doing this."

I, too, have my regular training buddies. During my preparation for the Los Angeles marathon, my friend Patty DiFalco—the cross-country coach for nearby Hofstra University—accompanied me most of the way for several of my long runs, even though she wasn't planning to do the marathon. Believe me, I was grateful for her company! Still, one day I faced a dilemma: because I was going on vacation the following weekend, I had a unusual Thursday long run scheduled (most runners go long on Sunday mornings, when it's cool and quiet and there's more time). It was a cold and windy January day, and none of my usual training partners were available. But I knew that I couldn't miss the long run. So I did something that I wouldn't necessarily recommend but that, to me, proves to what lengths we'll go to get the long runs in: I went out and rented the movie *Patton*, with George C. Scott, climbed on my treadmill, and ran from start to finish. I covered about 18 miles.

The movie was great. The run left me feeling like I had just been through a war. Your biomechanics when you run on a treadmill are a little different than when you're running outdoors, and so I was sore for a few days. I was happy when I entered that run in my training log, but I certainly would have preferred to have been outside on a crisp fall day or one of the first pleasant days of spring. That's when the long runs can actually become a pleasurable experience, if you let them. "Somewhere around 13 miles, you say 'Hey, I feel great. This is a beautiful day, I feel good,'" says Polansky. "And it's going to happen to you. You'll get one of those perfect days, not a cloud in the sky, temperature in the 50s and no wind, your body is recovering from the heat of summer or the cold of winter, and everything just clicks."

I'll let you in on a real secret about marathon training: on days like that, the long run is a beautiful thing.

CROSS-RUNNING, CROSS-TRAINING

Amby Burfoot wonders if marathon training will someday be refined to the point where a healthy person can actually complete a marathon on long runs every other weekend . . . and little else.

I'm not sure about that (although I'm sure somewhere out there, somebody has done just that). It is true, however, that for beginners, the emphasis must be on the long run. Most people have no problem with that concept; what they don't understand is the rest of the program, which emphasizes cross-training and rest.

This idea just doesn't sit well with some coaches and

runners. First-timers I talk to seem puzzled when I suggest to them that they can successfully complete a marathon by running no more than three or four times a week during the training period. A 1994 study from the University of Northern Iowa supports this less-is-more approach for novices. In the study, eighteen male and thirty-three female college students took part in an eighteen-week marathon training program. All were active and fit, but none had run a marathon before—in fact, almost all were running less than 10 miles per week when they started.

The subjects were divided into two groups. The high-mileage group averaged six workouts a week, their weekly mileage totals skyrocketing from 23 to 48. The low-mileage group trained only four days a week, going from 18 miles to 39. Their training mirrored a typical marathon program, with long runs in duration of up to two and a half hours.

At the end of the eighteen-week training period, both groups had lost body fat, increased muscle mass, improved their VO_2 max (a measure of the body's ability to use oxygen), and reduced their heart rates. Good outcomes, but interestingly enough, the improvements were identical in both groups. And so were the marathon times: males in both the high- and low-mileage groups had an average finishing time of 4:17 (with times ranging from 3:36 to 4:53); the women averaged 4:51 (the range was 3:51 to 6:32).

Although no one measured it, it's probably safe to say that the low-mileage group also had more time to pursue the rest of their lives during the training program—I would bet they also had more energy during their long runs—and recovered faster than those who had been pounding the pavement for 48 miles a week.

"The message for first-time marathoners is clear," concluded Owen Anderson, Ph.D., in an article on the study in *Running Research News*. "Capping four weekly workouts with a fifth or even sixth workout . . . is unlikely to help you at all."

The question remains: what should those three or four weekly workouts consist of? Well, for first-timers aiming simply to finish, the long run, as I've said, is the key. You could, and probably should, take it easy on the other two or three runs you do during the week, keeping the distances low and the pace comfortable. By "low" I mean only 3 to 4 miles at the beginning, when your long runs are no longer than 6 miles, and 5 to 6 miles later in the program, when your long runs are much longer. Depending on your background, your goals, and the marathon you're going to run, you might also want to consider using these shorter runs as opportunities to do a little so-called "quality" training. Here are some thoughts on your "cross-running" program.

SPEED WORK

We've said that time shouldn't be a goal in your first marathon. However, if you're a fast 10K runner looking to make the jump up to the marathon, you're probably going to ignore that advice. Which means you'll be doing some hard running as well as some long running. Track work—the quarter, half, and mile repeats (fast runs) that are the key to building speed at any distance—is demanding. So are the long runs. For the average first-time marathoner, doing both is an invitation to injury.

For that reason, Galloway advises beginning marathoners to avoid speed work and conserve most of their energy for the long runs. Others disagree: "Some faster running will help you do a more comfortable race," says Bakoulis. "It teaches you how to pace yourself and run more efficiently."

You don't need a track or a stopwatch for this kind of speed work—it's more like speed play, more commonly known to runners by its Swedish name, "fartlek." Simply take two- or three-minute intervals at a faster than normal pace during one of your shorter runs during the week. Or you can throw in a fartlek run on a weekend when you're not scheduled to do a long run. And if you don't want to count minutes, alternate hard and easy intervals between traffic lights or telephone poles. But do no more than three or four of these fast spurts during any one run.

HILL WORK

Sooner or later you're going to run into hills. When I did Los Angeles—which I had imagined was as flat as the streets are long—I was shocked to find fairly steep hills throughout the course. Living as I do on Long Island, I wasn't prepared for them—and it hurt. On the other hand, back in 1988, when I had done a great deal of my training in New York City's Central Park, a course renowned for its unrelenting hills, I was well prepared to run Connecticut's hilly Stamford Marathon. In fact, I believe that hill training was the reason I was able to cut nearly twenty minutes off my marathon time that year.

Recently, *Runner's World* columnist Joe Henderson tackled the issue of hills. A runner who had signed up for the *Charlotte Observer* Marathon had written him in a panic when she'd learned this was one of the hilliest courses on the East Coast. "What advice can you offer a first-time marathoner on a hilly course?" she asked.

"Don't fear or fight the uphills," Henderson wrote. "To use a driving or biking term, downshift into a slower climbing gear on the ascent. Then resume normal speed on the other side."

If you're worried about hills, it's advisable to find out how hilly the race you're planning to run is, so that it doesn't come as a surprise. Study the race application, call the race director. And then practice. Because hill running isn't just brute strength: it's technique.

Most runners, myself included, have a tendency to play Teddy Roosevelt. Every hill is San Juan Hill, and we want to *chaaaaarge* up to the top. It's much smarter and safer to play Eleanor Roosevelt—be diplomatic and flexible, and don't lose your composure. Shift gears going up, and don't get carried away by gravity going down. "Hold yourself back to save your legs from taking an awful pounding," says Henderson. "Keep the stride low and let the slightly bent knees act as shock absorbers."

Practice these hill techniques during one of your shorter weekly runs—either on your training course or on a treadmill where you can raise the incline. Henderson's letter writer did, and here's the postscript: "I followed your advice about working with the hills," she wrote him after the marathon. "My confidence was great and I knew without a doubt that I could have a strong finish. The hills were my favorite part of the course."

TUNE-UP RACES

As the weeks roll by in your training program and the big day looms larger and larger, you need to start getting yourself into a race mindset—or, at least, into the race atmosphere. For some runners, this is no problem. They race every weekend: they love the atmosphere, the camaraderie, the competitiveness.

I enjoy races, but truth be told, if I didn't have to cover them for *Newsday*, *Runner's World*, the *New York Running News*, or some other publication, I'd go to fewer. I much prefer the time I spend training on the roads with my friends. If you're like me, or if you've done a lot of your training alone, it is important that you do a couple of races before the marathon, for several reasons. First, races help you "psych" yourself up a little bit. Second, and more important, you'll get practice taking water and pacing yourself under race conditions, under which everybody tends to get a bit carried away the minute the gun goes off.

This is the time to see how you react to sports drinks before or during the race (we'll be talking more about that in chapter 7). This is the time to learn how to maintain pace discipline, to run within yourself. And if you are running against the clock, this is the time to see what you're capable of.

Some marathons have tune-up races built in as part of their schedule. For example, where I live, the Long Island Road Runners Club has a whole series of races of varying distances leading up to the Long Island Marathon in May. The New York City Marathon has a 15.4-mile tune-up race in

October—and, typical of Big Apple proportions, that race is probably bigger than most of the marathons in the country.

Tune-up races also provide excellent opportunities for runners to cover part of the course they'll run on race day. (In the New York tune-up, runners go twice over the marathon's last few miles in Central Park.) Depending on where you live and where you're going to be running your marathon, you should choose a race that to some extent duplicates the course you'll be running for some of the reasons cited above in the discussion of hill training. Nothing beats familiarity with a course, especially the last few miles in a marathon, when the only thing you care about seeing is the finish line!

If you don't normally race much, I'd recommend looking for a local 10K one or two weeks before your marathon. It will put you into the race environment, give you a chance to take fluids at water stops, let you practice your warm-up and cool-down routine, and above all, it will start to get you pumped up for the big day.

CROSS-TRAINING

As we saw in the Northern Iowa study, those who ran and ran didn't do any better than those who ran and rested. "Rest" during your marathon training program should include just that—days of complete rest, when you give your body a break. But for the sake of your program and your overall fitness, you should also be doing some form of cross-training. Bakoulis has written a whole book on this subject, and many shoe manufacturers have built fortunes on it, designing "cross-training" shoes that you can supposedly do everything in.

For the purposes of a marathon training program, though, cross-training means working out on days when you give your legs a rest from the pounding while still maintaining your fitness. What kind of cross-training is best for marathoners? We posed the question to one of the country's greatest cross-trainers: six-time Hawaii Ironman champion Mark Allen.

Allen, arguably the greatest endurance athlete in America, recommends two modes of cross-training for marathon runners. First, stationary biking: "It's good for recovery after long runs," he says. "It doesn't have to be intense or long. The idea is just to move the blood through your legs without putting any more impact on the joints."

Stationary biking sounds incredibly boring to some people, but not Allen: he makes his hour-long workouts interesting by listening to music as he rides and changing his riding pace. After a five-minute warm-up, he'll do twenty minutes of steady riding and then work with alternate legs—first pedaling with only the right leg, then with the left—or put in a few fast intervals. You can also just ride—either outdoors or indoors on a stationary bike—at a comfortable pace for thirty or forty minutes, if you prefer. Remember, the idea here is not to set cycling records. It's simply an alternate way to maintain daily fitness without putting too much stress on your legs.

Allen's favorite form of cross-training, particularly during or after marathon training, is swimming. "If you like to swim," he says, "that's the best recovery you can do. When I was training for the 1994 Berlin Marathon, that was what I loved to do most. There's something about the water temperature; it gets the blood flowing into the legs and cools you off."

If you're not a swimmer, there are still other ways you can get into the pool. I first discovered deep-water running several years ago, when I had a stress fracture. While training for Los Angeles, I renewed my pool membership because I remembered how soothing that water was, how it enabled me to get a good workout without feeling beat up. I made it a regular part of my training. Once a week, I got into the pool and did easy running for an hour, using a heart-rate monitor to make sure I was in my training zone (60–70 percent of your maximum heart rate, which is computed by subtracting your age from 220). Besides the novelty of being in a pool in the middle of January, the workouts were made more pleasant by the fact that a couple of friends who also owned flotation devices (such as wet belts and vests) would join me. Submerged up to our necks, we'd talk as we "ran" back and forth in our lane at the Hofstra University Swim Center. One time we went for an hour and a half—I could have logged it as a long run! (Some folks do. I've read about injured runners who did most of their training in the pool and were still able to complete their marathons.)

If you don't have a bike or access to a pool, there's still another form of cross-training you can employ: walking. Turn-of-the-century distance runners, such as the legendary Alfie Shrubb, incorporated walking into their running regimens. Unfortunately, the situation seems to have degraded today to the point that the two activities are pitted against each other; it's walking *versus* running, with advocates of one claiming that the other is less effective or harmful. Forget about that controversy—walking is a great exercise, and it's all the more appropriate as a form of cross-training if you're going to take regular walking breaks during your long runs. When you do, make sure you practice good fitness-walking form:

❦ Walk with your head up, chin parallel to the ground and ears lined up with your shoulders.

❦ Keep your buns tight (to keep the hips from rolling in and causing lower back pain).

❦ Maintain your natural stride length.

❦ Use your arms to go faster. Let them swing freely from the shoulders, not the elbows. And keep the arm swing asynchronous with your footstrike—when your left leg goes forward, your right arm swings forward, angling across the body slightly. Keep your hands cupped and hanging loose.

Try to maintain this form when you take walking breaks during your long runs. And, although we haven't discussed running form (under the presumption that you've been running for a year or so already), it's always good to keep in mind. For me, an easy way to maintain proper form is to recall this little rhyme as I'm running: hands down, shoulders back, hips forward, stay relaxed.

To that rhyme, we'll add this line, for first-time marathoners: "Keep your feet close to the ground . . . so after 26 miles, you'll still be around."

Remember that the idea of running is to go forward—not up. Your feet shouldn't rise more than an inch off the ground when you run, especially when you're running very long distances. Some veteran runners talk about doing the marathon "shuffle"—by this they mean that their gait is

Proper running form.

compact, economic, with low ground clearance. This conserves energy and reduces the likelihood of injuries resulting from the impact of your foot strikes.

WEIGHT TRAINING

Years ago, runners ran, lifters lifted, and never the twain would meet. That's changed. Even coaches like Galloway, who as recently as 1991 felt that runners didn't need to lift weights, have reconsidered. Now he and just about every other authority recommend that runners incorporate some form of resistance training into their regimens as a way to maintain upper-body form in a race and to help prevent injuries.

The debate arises over the type, frequency, and intensity of training. Some recommend highly sports-specific strengthening exercises for the legs and midsection. Others say just use light weights to work the upper body. I say, forget about your running for a minute. When you consider weight training, think instead about your overall health and fitness.

Over the last couple of years, researchers have found that regular resistance training—with free weights or machines—increases strength and stability and can also play an important role in preventing osteoporosis by increasing bone density and strength. Small wonder that the American College of Sports Medicine now recommends that all adults should include two sessions of resistance training as part of their minimum weekly exercise.

In other words, if you're not weight training, you should

be, regardless of whether you're running a marathon. You don't want to start power lifting during a marathon build-up program, but a couple of sessions a week—forty-five minutes or so of working all the major muscles groups—is a good investment of time and energy, not only for your race but for your future health. If you're not sure which exercises are best, or how to do them, you should find a certified personal trainer. Check at your local health club: ask for references and for certification, preferably from a nationally recognized certifying body, such as the American College of Sports Medicine (ACSM), the American Council of Exercise (ACE), or the Aerobics and Fitness Association of America (AFAA). Try to find a trainer who has had experience working with runners. Discuss your goals and ask him or her to develop a basic resistance program for you, showing you proper form on the equipment available to you, whether it's a pair of dumbbells for your home or the machines and free weights at your local gym. (Although it varies with trainer and location, the cost for an hour of personal training generally ranges from twenty-five to sixty dollars an hour.)

If you don't have the means or access to a personal trainer or gym, you can strengthen your body with these three basic exercises, using body weight as resistance.

1. Push-ups: Strengthens chest, shoulders, and arms. Start with the modified version: knees on the floor, ankles crossed. Keep your palms flat and slightly wider apart than shoulder width. Descend slowly and simultaneously touch your chest and hips to the floor. Push up, pause, repeat. When you can comfortably do standard push-ups, make sure you keep your back straight. (See opposite page.)

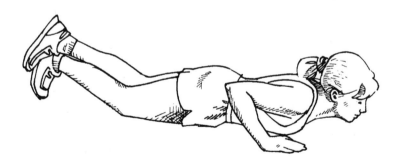

Figure 1: *Push-ups.*

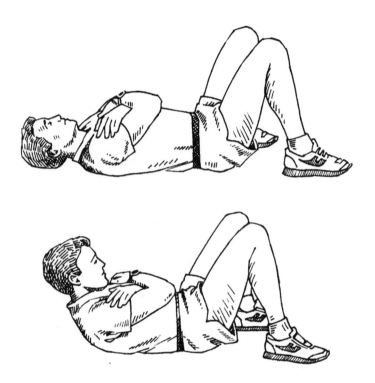

Figure 2: *Sit-ups.*

2. Crunches: This is the proper way to strengthen your midsection. Lie on your back with feet on a chair or flat on the floor, knees bent. Cross hands over chest and raise shoulders. Keep lower back flat on the floor.

3. Squats: These work your total lower body. With back straight, head up, hands out in front or at your sides for balance, slowly descend into a squatting position. Then push up from your heels, keeping your feet on the floor. (See opposite page.)

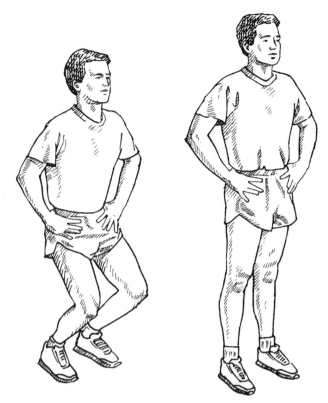

Figure 3: *Squats.*

Just make sure that you keep your weight workouts light during the peak of your running build-up period; and cut back your lifting during the last few weeks—after your last long run and before the marathon itself. Many people recommend that you stop lifting altogether before the race.

Sit down with the training log you should be keeping (which can be as simple as one of those calendars somebody gave you at Christmas that has been sitting around your house) and start penciling in some cross-training sessions around those all-important long runs. Resist the urge to run every day—and you'll be ready to run the race of your life.

6

Taking Care

In marathon training, patience is a virtue. "Trying to do too much, too soon . . . that's the biggest mistake people make," says Andres Rodriguez, M.D., the medical director for the New York City Marathon. In fact, he says, the majority of the approximately four thousand people his medical team treats every year at the world's largest 26.2-mile race are suffering either from exhaustion, because they pushed the pace, or dehydration, because they didn't want to waste precious seconds by pausing to take in fluids at the water stops along the course.

Bob Forster, physical therapist for Olympian Florence

Griffith Joyner, also sees the same mistake made every marathon season. "Some marathoners believe the best way to reach the finish line is by pushing their bodies right up until race day."

This book outlines a program in which the goal is to finish and feel good about it, not break records. You've been encouraged to run your long runs slowly, conservatively, with regular walking intervals. I've suggested that you compliment your weekly runs with cross-training and resistance work—good components for any fitness regimen.

There are other areas we need to talk about to round out your training and keep you fit and injury free for life—and the marathon.

The first is stretching. The second is sleep.

Traditionally, runners used to stretch before workouts. Some experts now believe that was a mistake because cold muscles don't stretch easily and are prone to pulls and tears. Nowadays, the thinking is that the best time to stretch is after a run—when the muscles are warm. Another change in the thinking on flexibility is the emergence of a new form of stretching: "AI" or assisted isolated stretching, in which the stretches are held for only a few seconds in order to contract the opposing muscle group.

The problem with AI is that you need access to coaches or trainers who know how to do it. Eventually, you can do it by yourself with a rope or chord for "assisting," but it takes some practice. Again, I'd recommend checking your local health club for certified AI instructors. In the meantime, most experts agree that there are still plenty of advantages to "static" stretching.

Gentle stretching, for the major muscle groups, means holding stretch positions for thirty to sixty seconds and never pushing to the point of pain. If you like to stretch, you can do it for hours and it's only going to help you keep your muscles loose during your marathon training. If you hate, it, like me, too bad: you still have to do it. But you can probably get away with the six basic stretches below recommended for runners by the American Physical Therapy Association. Try to do them every day—or at least after every run.

STRETCHING EXERCISES FOR RUNNERS

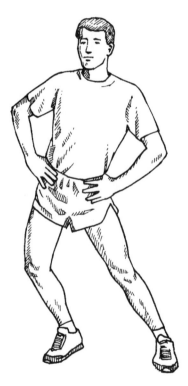

Inner Thigh Stretch

Stand with your feet pointed foward, about three feet apart. Bend your right knee. With hands on hips, shift your weight to the right side, keeping your knee directly over your right foot. Keep your left leg straight, and hold the stretch for five seconds. Stand up and repeat with the opposite leg.

(Figure 4)

Standing Quadriceps Stretch (Figure 5)

Standing straight, grasp the top of one foot behind your body with the opposite hand. Use the free hand to grasp a stationary surface for support. Gently pull the foot upward toward the buttocks, and hold the stretch for five seconds. Release the foot and repeat with the opposite leg.

(Figure 6)

Calf Muscle Stretch (Figure 6)

Stand facing a wall. Place both palms against the wall at shoulder level. Bend your right knee and move your left foot backward, keeping your left knee straight. With both heels flat, lean your trunk foward to stretch the left calf muscle. Hold for ten seconds. Relax and repeat with the opposite leg.

Hamstring Stretch (Figure 7)

Lift your right leg and rest your heel on a raised surface slightly below waist level. Keeping your right knee and back straight and your left leg relaxed, slowly lean forward from the hips and reach for your toes. Hold for ten seconds without bouncing. Repeat with your other foot. (See opposite page.)

(Figure 7)

Knees to Chest Stretch (Figure 8)

Lie on your back with your knees bent and your feet flat on the floor. Slowly lift one knee at a time and grasp your shins with both hands. Pull your knees gradually toward your chest until you feel a mild stretch in your lower back. Hold for ten seconds, then release and lower legs individually.

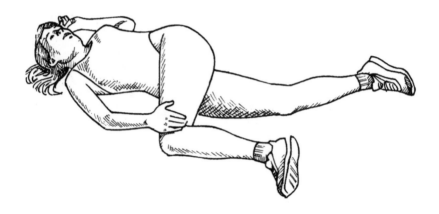

Lower Back Stretch (Figure 9)

Lie on your back with your right leg flat and left knee bent. Use your right hand to gently pull your left knee across your right leg and toward the ground, keeping your shoulders flat and tilting your head to the left. Hold the stretch for ten seconds and release, then repeat with the opposite leg and hand.

Do ten repetitions of each stretching exercise after running. None of these stretching exercises should cause pain or discomfort. If you feel pain, stop. These exercise tips are not a substitute for seeing a physical therapist or other health-care professional.

Another way to help your body and guard against injury is rest—or, to use Owen Anderson's wonderful term, "restoration," which makes us all sound like Renaissance masterpieces.

If you've been running for any length of time, you've probably heard the old saw about rest: that it's the most overlooked part of a training program. Nowhere is that more true than in a first-time marathon training program, in which you're subjecting your body and mind to new stresses, new challenges, and distances further than you've ever dreamed. To succeed, you need to handle your body with care. That means stretching, proper nutrition, and *rest*. Not only rest from running and training, but sleep (which shouldn't be too much of a problem during your training program). I think one of the best cures for insomnia might be marathon training. If you don't believe me, try staying up for the Late Show the night after a 20-miler.

Unlike stretching, sleep is rarely a problem for me. During most of my marathon training periods, I'll sleep eight to ten hours a night—sometimes even more. If you're generally a light sleeper, try to log a few more hours in the sack. Your body is going to need it. If you don't like the semi-comas that deep sleepers like myself fall into during our intense training periods, take naps.

There is good reason for you to get extra rest and take extra care during marathon training. Studies have shown that marathoners have depressed immune systems soon after their races. It's common for marathoners to talk about the prerace "cold." I think some of this can be avoided by taking care of yourself and not overdoing it. Again, although one case in point doesn't prove all that much, I will say that while training for my eighth marathon I followed a program similar to the one in this book—and was as healthy as a horse. Why? Well, one reason is that I rested more and ran a little less. I also took more vitamin supplements than I did in the past—particularly the so-called antioxidants, such as vitamins C and E (more about that in the next chapter).

I also did not suffer any significant injury during my training—just a little muscle soreness. And one thing that saved me from that ailment was a weekly session with a licensed massage therapist.

Massage is another controversial issue. Many members of the medical community still question its value. And although independent research on its effectiveness has produced mixed findings, most top runners—most top athletes in almost every sport, for that matter—are now making sports massage a part of their regular "bodywork." If you can afford it (the average cost is twenty-five dollars for a half hour, fifty dollars for an hour), I recommend getting a massage after each long run. Just make sure you have a licensed massage therapist. If you live in a state where they're not licensed, check references; make sure they've worked with athletes, preferably runners, before.

Besides the healing benefits of massage, including increased circulation and lactic acid and other waste removal from muscles, there's another plus: it's very relaxing. Think of it as your body's reward after a long run.

OVERTRAINING

As mentioned earlier, the whole philosophy of the Galloway program is moderation. Still, overtraining is a very real possibility in marathon preparation. Be alert to the warning signs (as compiled by Dr. Neil F. Gordon at the Cooper Institute for Aerobics Research):

❦ Changes in your sleep patterns, especially insomnia

❦ Longer healing periods for minor cuts and scratches

❦ A fall in blood pressure and dizziness when getting up from a prone or seated position

❦ A gradual loss of weight in the absence of dieting or increased physical activity

❦ A leaden or sluggish feeling in your legs during exercise

❦ Impaired mental acuity and performance or inability to concentrate

❦ An increase in your resting heart rate (recorded early in the morning) by more than ten beats per minute

❦ Excessive thirst and fluid consumption at night

❦ Lethargy, listlessness, and tiredness

❦ Loss of appetite

❦ Sluggishness that persists for more than twenty-four hours after a workout

While there are others on Dr. Gordon's list, these are more or less the classic signs of overtraining. If you have several of these symptoms, and particularly if they are persistent, cut back a little. Examine your training log and your progress, and see where you might be doing too much. Take one full rest day a week, if you aren't doing so already. Whatever you do, don't ignore these signs. Because when your race day arrives, you want to be at the starting line feeling good, not at home with the flu or nursing an injury.

Be alert to the symptoms of overtraining, get your rest, and you'll get to the finish line.

GETTING PROPERLY EQUIPPED

SHOES

*My friend Jim Fishman, a Manhattan publishing execu*tive, tells a story about shoes and marathon running that should be instructive to all of us.

In 1985, Fishman was training for the New York City Marathon. While on a trip to Maine in early fall, he stopped at an outlet center and bought, at a substantial discount, what he thought was a duplicate pair of the training shoes he'd been using all along. The sales clerk told him it was the same shoe. It wasn't. In the six months since he'd originally bought those shoes, the design had changed slightly but significantly. Fishman didn't realize this until the worst moment possible: twenty miles into the race. "I was in such pain," he recalls. "I couldn't figure out why, until I realized that it was all in the soles of my feet."

The new design—and remember, running-shoe companies change models and designs like you change socks—had less padding in the soles. Had Fishman stuck with the shoe he used all along—and bought that shoe in a running-apparel store—he probably wouldn't have had the problem. "I saved twenty dollars," he says, "And I paid for it with twenty miles of pain."

Fishman's story teaches us two important lessons. First, your shoes are the only equipment you really need to run a marathon, so don't skimp on the time or money it will take to get the right pair. Second, don't vary your routine late in the game (a point we'll get back to in chapter 8).

So how should you choose the proper shoes for running a marathon? It's easy. "Use the ones you're used to running in," says Bob Cook, owner of The Runner's Edge, a runningshoe and -apparel store in Farmingdale, New York.

Don't use a lighter racing shoe for the marathon: it may save you a couple of seconds in a 10K race, but it won't provide adequate protection for the average runner over 26.2 miles. If you do want to choose a new shoe, make sure you get a pair that has plenty of cushioning and stability. And wear them during your long runs. Same thing with your socks.

It used to be said that you should buy shoes a half or full size larger when you're planning to run a marathon. The thinking was that your feet swelled up so much during the race that your regular size would cause discomfort. Cook discounts that. "If they're properly sized," he says, "you'll have no problem." To ensure proper fit, he recommends using the standard "thumbnail test": if there's a thumbnail's width between your toes and the tips of your shoes, you're okay.

I ignored this advice one year and foolishly bought a

pair of shoes that were my size, but turned out to be just a tad too small (I didn't even do the thumbnail test). I broke in this new pair of shoes during a 15-mile training run with a friend. It was one of the singularly most painful experiences of my life—worse than any marathon. I finished with the laces undone and the tongue flopping out—anything to give my aching feet a release. When I was done I threw them against the garage door of my friend's house. I would have probably set fire to them if he didn't stop me.

Get the picture? You want your doggies to be comfortable during your marathon. Make sure your toenails are cut and filed before long runs and prior to the race (imagine having a hangnail for twenty miles). Cook recommends socks that wick the moisture away; avoid cotton, which tends to hold moisture.

Some runners tend to hold on to their shoes for too long. While you don't want to be breaking in a brand new pair of shoes on marathon day, you don't want to toe the line with a beat-up old pair, either. Cook recommends buying the shoes you'll actually run in about a month prior to the race. And make sure you do at least one long run in them, so you can see how they feel after a couple of hours or so.

Finally, when you've found the pair that's right for you, and you've logged some miles and a long run or two in them, stick by them. Don't change them on a whim a week before the race just because you saw a pair in a store window that had spiffier colors or a cooler design . . . or, as in the case with Jim Fishman, a lower price tag.

Stay loyal to the shoes that work for you and you won't go wrong . . . at least from the ankles down.

HEART MONITORS

In the two years since I wrote The Essential Runner, *heart* monitors have become an increasingly common sight on the roads. There are lots of good reasons to run with a monitor: it helps you avoid running too fast and, sometimes, running too slow. If you already run with one, there's certainly no need to change your habits when training for the marathon. You might even find that it makes good company and may help keep you going nice and slow during your long runs.

But you don't have to run with a heart monitor in order to run well. Many runners, myself included, run just fine without them. They are a useful tool for many; but don't let anyone tell you they are essential for every runner.

Because this is a book about the essentials and because the heart monitor is a separate topic in and of itself, I'd recommend that if you're interested in learning more about them, consult one of the several books and booklets devoted to heart monitors. Coach Roy Benson's *Precision Running*, a concise forty-five-page guide, covers the basics of heart-monitor training and use for runners. It's published by Polar Heart Monitors and sells for four dollars in most running-shoe stores. You can also purchase one through Polar: call (800) 262-7776 or write Polar CIC, Inc., 99 Seaview Blvd., Port Washington, NY 11050. For a more comprehensive treatment, see *The Heart Rate Monitor Book* by Sally Edwards (Sacramento: Fleet Feet Press, 1992) and *Heart Monitor Training for the Compleat Idiot*, by John L. Parker (Tallahassee: Cedarwinds Press, 1993).

Eyewear

Another new accessory frequently seen on the roads are sunglasses or, in the new parlance of the apparel business, "protective eyewear." I'm convinced that most of the runners who wear shades want to look cool. But more and more people believe there are good, sound reasons for wearing sunglasses while you run that have nothing to do with finish line photos. "I think people forget how important it is to protect your eyes," says Cook, referring particularly to the sun's damaging UV rays. Cheap sunglasses don't offer this protection. So if you're going to get a pair, look for those with UV protection. Although good glasses start at forty dollars, some of the brand name eyewear now goes for ninety to one hundred dollars.

Some research also shows that wearing glasses can relax you a little bit—simply because you're not squinting as much. So maybe you not only look cooler, you are cooler!

Chronometers

Time and speed have been deemphasized throughout this book. Still, you've probably been wearing your running watch—or chronometer—to keep track of your pace or your walking intervals. I could tell you that one of the best things you could do to relax for your first marathon is simply leave your watch in the hotel or at home on race day, but that would be a bit hypocritical. I've always worn a watch—and in marathons when I was shooting for a time, it was critical.

So if you want to wear your watch on race day, do. But don't wear one you've never used before or aren't familiar with. That may sound obvious but in 1990, en route to the Chicago Marathon, I accidentally grabbed a watch I don't frequently use. Five miles into the race I looked down and saw a blank face. So there I was, running along the roads of the Windy City, frantically pushing buttons as the watch beeped, changed modes, lit up—everything it could possibly do except get back to elapsed time. I probably finished that race with my watch counting laps from a workout in July, or displaying the correct time in Cairo. Needless to say, I'm still not sure what happened—but I know that it made for a frustrating experience.

If You Do Get Hurt

As a runner, you ought to know this drill by heart: RICE—rest, ice, compression, elevation: the standard first-aid formula for running injuries. If problems persist, cut back or stop your training and see a doctor. Don't assume that a trip to the doctor's office means the end of your marathon. Most marathon injuries are overuse injuries, which will sometimes respond with a few days of rest, some specific stretches, or a simple adjustment to your shoes or orthotics.

While injuries are a part of marathon running, they can be avoided. "The majority of marathon training injuries are the result of programs that aren't of long duration or that don't allow for enough rest," says Dr. Edward Fryman, podiatrist and medical director for the Long Island Marathon.

You can't prepare for the marathon in eight weeks, or by trying to cram in too many long runs in too short a time, or by doing too few long runs without dramatically increasing the chances of getting hurt. That's why the program outlined in this book is so conservative—and why it's got such a high success rate. The runners who follow this schedule generally stay healthy.

Still, you're asking a lot from your body, so it's important to recognize the most common types of "overuse" injuries and how to treat them.

ACHILLES TENDENITIS   This is pain and inflammation in the large tendon that connects the heel and calf muscle. It's a result of overwork by the calf muscle, which shifts much of the burden of running to the Achilles. Because this condition is often found among runners who increase their mileage too quickly, it's one that first-time marathon runners should be especially alert to.

Treatment: Rest, ice, and anti-inflammatory drugs will help. Stretching the calves can also help here, as can proper shoes. Dr. Joe Ellis, in his book *Running Injury Free* (see Appendix) recommends looking for a pair with flexible forefeet that can lessen the load on the Achilles.

CHONDROMALACIA   This is a classic running knee injury— a softening of the cartilage under the kneecap, causing soreness and often swelling. Dave Kuehls pointed out in a *Runner's World* article on common running injuries that this condition is often caused by excessive pronation (when the foot rotates too far inward) or a muscular imbalance between the quadriceps and hamstrings of the legs.

Treatment: Ice and rest are recommended, followed by strengthening exercises for the quadriceps, such as leg extensions on a weight machine.

PLANTAR FASCIITIS   Ellis calls this "The most talked-about, most written-about and possibly most dreaded injury in running." It's an inflammation of the plantar fascia—a long fibrous band of tissue that runs along the bottom of the foot.

Treatment: As Ellis points out, it's almost impossible to resolve this issue without proper treatment. Simply changing your footwear doesn't help. What does is ice, orthotics (specially molded shoe inserts, prescribed by a podiatrist, to correct biomechanical problems), or over-the-counter— or prescribed—anti-inflammatory drugs.

Good preventive measures include calf-strengthening and stretching exercises, and an exercise for strengthening the muscles of foot that simply involves picking up marbles or golf balls between your toes and the ball of your foot.

SHIN-SPLINTS   Sports medicine types disdain this term, because it really refers to a number of lower leg problems, the most common of which is tendenitis of the lower leg. Causes of this problem—which presents itself as an aching or throbbing pain along the inside of the knee—can vary, but is often found among runners who increase their mileage too quickly.

Treatment: Again, stretching and strengthening exercises can help, as will rest.

STRESS FRACTURE   This is an actual break in the bone, usually occurring in the feet, shins, or thigh, and sometimes in the ankle or pelvis. These typically begin as a dull ache but can develop into a sharp, persistent pain, especially during running.

Treatment: Because stress fractures occur when the bone can no longer withstand the increased pressure placed on it, the source of the pressure must be eliminated. That means no running, generally for six to eight weeks, while the bone heels. Wearing a cast is not necessary in most cases, but finding an alternate form of nonweight-bearing exercise is.

While you should be alert to the symptoms of injuries, don't forget that some aches or pains are to be expected. If you feel some pain or discomfort during a training run, don't panic. "The first thing to do is to slow your pace down a bit," says Fryman. "If it persists, stop and walk for a few minutes, then resume running. Then, if it still hurts, the best thing to do is turn around and go home, and give it some rest."

Take a couple of days off, RICE your injury, and stretch that body. If it persists for more than a few days, get help from a sports podiatrist or orthopedic specialist or physician (preferably one who runs or knows something about running). Massage therapists, physical therapists, and chiropractors can also be helpful.

Most of the problems that Fryman sees occur in the last few weeks before the marathon—these are often the people who have tried to do too much too soon. Don't be one of those who try to play catch-up and ends up on the sidelines. Plan your program realistically, build up your mileage gradually, and you should be ready to roll on marathon day.

And if a doctor tells you that your injury requires you to bag the marathon this time, heed the advice. There are lots of marathons all year long. You can always come back in a few months. Remember that virtue called patience.

7

Fuel for the Long Run

Under any circumstances, eating well is key to maintaining a healthy body and a clear mind. But marathon running pushes you, mind and body, making diet a critical element for success.

Eating well doesn't start and end with a bowl of pasta the night before the marathon. It begins during training and extends throughout the race. In fact, the eating habits you develop during marathon training can benefit you way beyond the glory of race day. They can be a boon to you for the rest of your life.

THE TRAINING DIET

A good training diet is not an extreme, potion-loaded plan. Rather, it is consistent with everyday healthy eating, with a few alterations. Like any sensible diet, this one is grounded in the basics, so I'll start off here with a sort of Nutrition 101 overview, covering the essential nutrients and how they fit into the big picture.

CALORIES

Calories are what our bodies burn for fuel. They are *energy.* And as an endurance runner you burn a lot more of them than do sedentary folk, anywhere from 2,500 to 4,000 calories a day.

For a rough idea of how many calories you need during training, multiply your weight in pounds by 15. Then add 100 calories for every mile you run a day. Use that number as a guide, but don't go nuts counting calories. If you eat according to your appetite and you maintain your weight, you are getting enough.

All of the calories in food come from one of three sources: carbohydrates (4 calories per gram), protein (4 calories per gram), or fat (9 calories per gram). Most experts agree that a balanced, high-carbohydrate diet with about 60 percent of the calories from carbohydrates, 15–20 percent from protein, and 20–25 percent from fat is best for most active people.

CARBOHYDRATES

Carbohydrates, affectionately referred to as carbs by fitness buffs, are a bigwig in the world of sports nutrition. They are the main fuel for exercising muscles, and our bodies can only store a small amount (in the form of glycogen), so a steady dietary supply is critical.

Carbohydrates come in two forms, complex and simple. Complex carbohydrates are found in the foods that my grandma called starches—breads, rice, pasta, and other grains. They are packed with vitamins, minerals, and fiber and should make up the bulk of your carbohydrate intake. Simple carbohydrates, commonly known as sugars, are best obtained from unrefined sources, like fruit, where they come with lots of vitamins and minerals. Refined sugars, found in soft drinks and sweets, are practically void of any nutrients besides calories. Vegetables are a nutrient-packed source of both simple and complex carbohydrates.

PROTEIN

Most runners don't think protein is something they need to be concerned with; they leave that to the weight lifters. But runners who follow the high-carb mantra to extremes and ignore protein may wind up protein deficient, with symptoms including fatigue, muscle wasting, and a weakened immune system.

As it turns out, endurance trainers need just as much protein as weight lifters, because protein not only builds muscle but is burned as fuel during long bouts of exercise. To keep your body running smoothly, during training aim to get about .6 grams of protein per pound of body weight. That's about 80 grams per day for a woman and 95 grams per day for a man.

Luckily, even with those higher requirements it is easy to get enough protein with a balanced and varied diet. Meat, fish, poultry, dairy, and eggs are excellent protein sources. Beans, nuts, and grains are good sources too, so even strict vegetarians can get the protein they need by eating a variety of foods. Check the box below for the protein content of some foods.

PROTEIN CONTENT OF FOODS

FOOD	AMOUNT	PROTEIN (G)
Poultry, Fish, Meat	3 oz cooked	21
Milk, Yogurt	1 cup	8
Peanut Butter	2 Tbs	8
Pasta	1 cup cooked	7
Beans, Tofu	½ cup	7
Cheese	1 oz	7
Egg	1 large	7
Bread	1 slice	3

Fat

There has been a lot of press about the deleterious effects of eating too much fat. And it's true, high-fat diets have been linked to obesity, heart disease, diabetes, and cancer, among other ailments. But fat isn't all bad. A small amount is essential in the human diet, and fats are the only food sources of certain vitamins, like E and K. Fat also makes you feel satisfied, and because it is so calorically dense (with more than twice as many calories per gram as protein or carbs), eating enough helps you meet your increased caloric needs during training.

To make fat work for you, not against you, remember these two words: balance and quality. Keep your fat intake in balance by getting about 25 percent of your calories from fat. To figure out how many grams that is, multiply your total caloric needs by .25 and divide by 9. On average that comes to about 60 grams per day for a woman and 75 grams per day for a man.

Make the most out of the fat in your diet by opting for quality sources. That is, when adding fat to foods use "good" fats like olive oil and other unsaturated vegetable oils, instead of "bad" fats like butter, cream, and hydrogenated oils. And try to use your fat allowance on nutritious foods like nuts, nut butters, and avocados, as opposed to fried foods, fatty cuts of meats, cakes, and candy.

Vitamins and Minerals

Most runners want to know which vitamins they need to take to perform their best and recover quickly. The answer, simply, is none. A study published in the *American Journal of Clinical Nutrition* had the "overriding conclusion" that "vitamin and mineral supplements are unnecessary in athletes consuming well-balanced diets," and most experts agree.

The key phrase in that last sentence is "well-balanced diets." Because while taking supplements is not critical, getting enough of all essential vitamins and minerals is. The best way to do that is by eating a variety of nutritious foods.

Many runners believe they need to take supplements because training hikes up their nutrient requirements. It's true that endurance training boosts the need for some vitamins and minerals, but needs don't increase as much as some supplement marketers would like you to believe. And because vigorous exercisers have to eat more food, they get more nutrients anyway.

The antioxidant vitamins (vitamin C, vitamin E, and beta-carotene) have been making headlines lately, as they are thought to have a role preventing cancer, heart disease, aging, and even muscular soreness. While researchers know that these vitamins protect cells from harmful toxins, they are still debating the merits of antioxidant supplements. But just about everyone agrees that it's a plus to eat plenty of antioxidant-rich foods, primarily fruits and vegetables. Besides providing antioxidants, fruits and vegetables contain a wealth of other protective factors that scientists are just beginning to identify.

Although deemed unnecessary, supplements are popular among people with well-balanced diets as a sort of "health insurance." If you want to cover yourself, a daily multivitamin with minerals is a good way to go. Also, an antioxidant supplement with 250–500 mg of vitamin C,

100-400 I.U. of vitamin E, and 15,000-25,000 I.U. of betacarotene is considered safe and could be beneficial. If you are a strict vegetarian or you have other dietary constraints, you may need supplements and should consult with a qualified nutritionist for the best plan. Just remember, when it comes to vitamins and minerals, too much can be just as harmful as too little, and no pill can take the place of a healthy diet.

WATER

Water is often called the forgotten nutrient because it is so commonly overlooked. But for marathoners, overlooking water can be fatal. Water is such a critical nutrient for long-distance runners that it gets a whole section of its own called THINK DRINK later in the chapter.

ENOUGH WITH THE NUMBERS, WHAT'S FOR LUNCH?!

So now you have the basics, and with that a lot of numbers floating around in your head—numbers of calories, grams of fat, and so on. Those numbers are a good point of reference, but no one wants to sit down to dinner, calculator in hand, figuring out grams of this and percentages of that between bites of salad. Thankfully, there is no need to, because the following food guide takes all those numbers and spins them down into a simple eating plan. By following this plan, you will wind up with a balanced, high-carbohydrate diet, with adequate protein, vitamins, and minerals to keep you running your best.

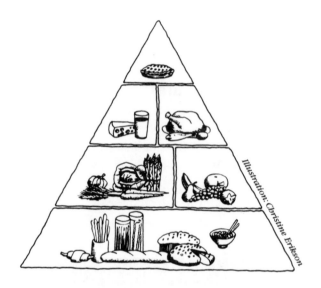

Illustration: Christine Erikson

THE FOOD GUIDE PYRAMID

The Food Guide Pyramid, developed by the U.S. Department of Agriculture, is a modern version of the well-known but outmoded four food groups. The pyramid has five food groups: bread, vegetables, fruit, milk, and meat. Each group is an important part of a good diet, but each is not needed in equal quantities, as emphasized by the pyramid's shape. The bread group is the base of the triangle and the cornerstone of a high-carbohydrate diet. The vegetable and fruit groups are the next largest groups, and the milk and meat groups are the smallest in the picture. At the very tip of the triangle is a section for fats and sweets, which should be eaten sparingly.

BREAD This group includes bread, rice, cereal, pasta, and other grains. During training, aim to get about 12 to 17 servings per day in this group. This may seem like a lot at first glance, but a serving is small: ½ cup of cooked pasta, rice, or grains, or 1 slice of bread. So a typical bowl of pasta, which holds about 2 cups, adds up to 4 servings.

VEGETABLES Besides leafy greens, broccoli, carrots, and the like, this group includes starchy vegetables like potatoes and corn. And although they are usually placed in the meat group because of their high protein content, I like to include beans and dried peas here, because they are starchy vegetables too.

A good training diet has 5-6 servings in this group per day, with a serving being one cup of raw leafy vegetables, ½ cup of cooked vegetables, ½ cup cooked beans, or ¾ cup of vegetable juice.

FRUIT Aim to get 5-9 servings of fruit each day during training. One medium-sized fruit, ½ cup of chopped or cooked fruit, and ¾ cup of fruit juice each count as a serving.

MILK This group includes milk, yogurt, and cheese. Four to five servings a day should do it, with a serving being 1 cup of milk or yogurt or 1½ ounces of cheese.

MEAT Besides meat, this group includes poultry, fish, eggs, nuts, and seeds. If you are a vegetarian, switch beans, tofu, and dried peas to this group from the vegetable group to help ensure you get the protein you need. Aim to get 5–13 servings a day, with a serving being 1 ounce of cooked meat, poultry, or fish, ½ cup of cooked beans, 1 egg, or 2 tablespoons of peanut butter.

The recommended ranges of servings for each food group have been modified here to account for increased needs during training. Where you fit into the range depends on your caloric needs as indicated in the chart below. To use the pyramid after you've run the marathon, decrease the number of servings in each group proportionally to meet your lower caloric needs.

SERVING RANGES

FOOD GROUP	SERVING SIZE	Calories			
		SERVINGS PER DAY *Broken Down by Daily Total Calories*			
		2,500	3,000	3,500	4,000
Grains	1 oz or ½ cup	12	12	15	17
Vegetables	½ cup	5	5	6	6
Fruit	1 fruit or ½ cup	5	6	8	9
Milk	1 cup	4	4	5	5
Meat	1 oz	5	7	10	13

You may want to keep a daily record of servings you eat in each group until you get a sense how it feels to eat this way. Or simply try to shape each meal according to the pyramid. For example, a typical American meal might consist of a large piece of chicken with a little rice and vegetable on the side. A more pyramid-like meal would have a larger portion of rice, mixed with plenty of vegetables, and a few small pieces of chicken.

The Food Guide Pyramid shapes a healthy diet, but a key dimension to eating well is not apparent in it: the selections made within each group. Technically, a donut and a piece of whole wheat bread both count as a serving in the bread group, but everyone knows that they are not the same nutritionally.

To truly eat well, opt for wholesome, lowfat, unprocessed foods as much as possible. Try to stay away from packaged foods, which can have an ingredient list that reads like a chemistry textbook. Choose whole-grain breads and cereals, lean cuts of meat, poultry without the skin, and low-fat milk products. Avoid baked goods with lots of added fat or sugar and processed, high-fat meats. Go for foods that are steamed, broiled, or baked as opposed to fried. And stick to vegetable-based sauces and soups instead of those with butter or cream.

That doesn't mean hot dogs and cheese balls are off limits. There is always room for some of any food in a well-rounded diet. Just keep those foods as "occasionals" and make the better choices the backbone of your diet.

BUT WON'T CARBOHYDRATES MAKE ME FAT?

If you hesitate to follow a high-carbohydrate diet because you've read that carbohydrates make you fat, don't worry.

Only a very small percentage of people have a problem with carbohydrates per se. The truth is, eating too many calories of anything leads to weight gain. Many high-carbohydrate products, promoted as "fat-free," are loaded with refined sugar and calories so, naturally, overeating them will make you fat. If you stick to unprocessed foods and follow serving guidelines, a high-carbohydrate diet will keep you in good shape.

If you are trying to shed pounds during training, be sure not to restrict your calories excessively. Chances are, the increase in running mileage alone will make you lose weight, and dieting could backfire by hampering your workouts. At most, avoid high-fat and sugary foods and aim for no more than one to two pounds of weight loss per week.

EATING ON THE GO

All of this sounds great on paper, you're saying. But how do you expect me to eat well when I barely have time to breathe regularly? Luckily, you don't have to sit down to three squares a day to get the nutrition you need. Many busy athletes fuel up by "grazing" throughout the day.

To keep grazing healthy and avoid vending-machine roulette, be sure you have access to the right foods. Stock up at home and at the office with healthy stuff you can eat while you work or as you dash out the door. Individual yogurts, precut veggies, fruit, cans of tuna, instant bean soups, whole-grain rolls and crackers, and half a sandwich are all easily munched on the go. Sure, it's good to sit down to a full-fledged meal when you can, but sometimes it's just not possible. In those cases, sensible snacking is a high-energy alternative.

Energy Bars and Shakes

When you are faced with a time crunch you may look toward sports bars and shakes for convenience. These products are okay once in a while, but don't rely on them. Less-processed foods, like some of the options described above, can be just as convenient and more nutritious.

When opting for a sports bar, look for one that contains wholesome ingredients like whole grain oats or figs and has less than 25 percent of its calories from fat. Some sports bars have so much fat and refined sugar they are really just glorified candy bars. And don't be fooled by exotic ingredients that claim to increase energy and performance. There is no one food or substance with such magical properties.

Many athletes like to drink their meals, especially before a run, because liquid meals are digested faster than solid ones. Instead of relying on powders, try blending low-fat milk, your favorite fruit, and some cereal or graham crackers for an easy, nutritious liquid meal.

Can I Take Something to Make Me Run Better?

An array of products on the market claim to boost performance overnight or give runners an extra edge. Protein powders, L-carnitine, bee pollen, ginseng, and green algae have all been promoted as such, but there is no solid evidence to support their use. Studies do show that caffeine (in doses equaling the amount in two to three cups of coffee) can improve endurance. But caffeine can also cause anxiety, gastrointestinal cramping, and dehydration, so the risks of using it may well outweigh the benefits. As a rule, if a product sounds too good to be true, it probably is.

THINK DRINK

Long-distance running places huge demands on fluid needs, making drinking enough a number-one priority for marathoners. When you're running, your body generates heat, which it dissipates by sweating. If the water lost to sweat is not replaced, the body's cooling system falters, and problems ensue. Symptoms of dehydration include fatigue, lightheadedness, muscle cramps, increased heart rate, and, in extreme cases, loss of consciousness and death.

Fortunately, dehydration is easily avoided with some vigilant imbibing. But don't wait until you feel thirsty to say "bottoms up." The human thirst mechanism is unreliable. It doesn't kick in until the body is already somewhat dehydrated.

To tell if you are drinking enough check the color and quantity of your urine. Clear, frequent urine indicates good hydration, whereas amber colored, scant urine means you need to drink more. Be aware, however, that caffeine and alcohol can skew this simple indicator. They are diuretics, which dehydrate, making urine clear and copious at first, but later dark and scant.

By drinking enough to keep your urine clear throughout the day you can avoid "catch-up" drinking right before you run. Loading up on fluids can't make up for a day's worth of water loss anyway, and it could give you stomach cramps. To approach a workout in the best possible condition, a well-hydrated person should drink about two cups of fluid twenty minutes to an hour before exercising.

It is also important to replenish fluids during your runs. The American College of Sports Medicine recommends drinking 4 to 6 ounces of fluid every fifteen to twenty minutes during exercise. To figure out your individual needs more exactly, weigh yourself right before and right after you work out. Your weight difference is the amount of water you've lost to perspiration. For every pound shed plan to drink 16 ounces (2 cups) of water over the course of your next run. Because the rate of perspiration varies with training intensity and the weather, reassess fluid needs as these conditions change.

Now that you know how much to drink, the question is what to drink. The ideal hydrating drink is water: it is absorbed quickly, has no calories, and costs little or nothing. But any beverage that doesn't contain caffeine or alcohol counts toward hydration. Pure juices are more nutritious than soft drinks, but both are fine hydrators. Try sparkling water flavored with fruit juice or herbal iced tea as a quenching alternative. The idea is to drink what tastes good, so you drink more. Ideally, drinks should be consumed at refrigerator temperature (40° F), because cool beverages are absorbed faster.

SPORTS DRINKS

Sports drinks are a good choice, especially during a long run. Along with fluid, they provide carbohydrates, which have been shown to increase stamina when consumed during bouts of exercise lasting an hour or more. Other beverages have carbohydrates too, but sports drinks, which are 6–7 percent carbohydrate, are easily digested, whereas juices and soft drinks, which are 11–12 percent carbohydrate, are more concentrated and likely to cause cramping when ingested during a run. Also, a recent study published in the *International Journal of Sports Medicine* shows that during exercise, the type of carbohydrate used in sports drinks (glucose) is more efficiently utilized than that in fruit juice (fructose). But don't buy into the idea that you can't make it through a marathon with out an expensive beverage. If sports drinks don't agree with you or you just prefer not to spend the money on them, fruit juice diluted fifty-fifty with water or herbal iced tea with honey are acceptable alternatives. You can also stick to ever-reliable water and nibble fruit or crackers on the road for carbohydrates.

EATING BEFORE, DURING, AND AFTER TRAINING RUNS

T alking about sports drinks leads in to the all-important topic of carbohydrate management. As I mentioned before, carbohydrates are the main fuel for exercising muscles, and stores of this valued fuel, called glycogen, don't last very long—only an hour and a half or so. Therefore, much of what you eat before, during, and after you run involves maximizing glycogen stores and keeping blood sugar steady so glycogen is conserved.

Before

Your prerun meal should provide a sustained flow of carbohydrates and be easily digested. The latest evidence shows that foods like rice, corn, lentils, and pasta, oatmeal high in carbohydrates but with a relatively low glycemic index (that is, they don't cause a rapid rise in blood sugar) are the best choice. They trickle fuel into your blood gradually, as opposed to high glycemic foods like sugary drinks, sweets, and, to a lesser degree, bread and potatoes, which give you an initial carbohydrate boost but can subsequently cause a dip in blood sugar. Keep prerun meals low in fat, and allow enough time for proper digestion. That's three to four hours for a regular meal, two to three hours for a small meal, and up to an hour for a snack.

During

Consuming carbohydrates during long runs slows glycogen burnout and in turn delays fatigue and enhances performance. For runs lasting an hour or more, aim to ingest 40-70 grams of carbohydrate an hour, which is 160-280 calories' worth. This is where sports drinks do their job best, but choose whatever source you find most convenient and easily digested. Bananas, orange slices, crackers, and pretzels are runners' old standbys.

Although 40-70 grams of carbohydrate an hour is considered optimal, most athletes have a hard time ingesting that much when they run. In fact, many runners don't ingest carbohydrates while running at all. All things considered, the best advice is to be aware of what is optimal and to try to reach that goal based on your individual tolerance.

After

Glycogen stores are most readily replaced within two hours of a workout, so as soon as possible after you run aim to get about 300 calories' worth of carbohydrates. As far as beverages go, fruit juice and soft drinks are more efficient postexercise replenishers than diluted sports drinks. Either three cups of juice or six cups of a sports drink will cover you. Or if you prefer to drink water and eat your postrun carbs, a banana and half a bagel will meet your needs for the first two hours after running. Then, plan to have a high-carbohydrate meal within the next two hours to completely restore glycogen.

There is no need to take any special electrolyte supplement to replace those lost during a run. Sodium and potassium, the two electrolytes that are of most concern for marathoners, are easily replenished during the postrun meal. During the marathon, if you drink only water there is a small chance of becoming sodium depleted, but if you nibble a salty snack or sip on sports drinks during the race, you will prevent any imbalance.

Fine-Tuning

Use training as an opportunity to experiment with what drink and snack combinations work best for you before, during, and after running, so there are no surprises on marathon day. You can call race headquarters and find out what they'll be giving away on race day and practice drinking it in training. Everybody is different. What one person finds easily digested and energizing can cause cramping in someone else. Training is a time to listen to your body and fine-tune your habits so everything runs smoothly during the event.

PREPPING FOR THE BIG TWO-SIX

ONE WEEK AND COUNTING

The week before the marathon, as you taper your training you also need to make some adjustments in your diet. Running less means you need fewer calories, so keep up the pyramid-style eating, but reduce your caloric intake by 100 calories for every mile you drop from your schedule.

Three to four days before the big event you'll want to focus on increasing your carbohydrate intake so that it is 65–70 percent of your total calories. By boosting carbohydrate intake and resting your muscles you supersaturate your glycogen stores, so you will have more endurance for the long run. Increasing carbohydrates to this level means substituting some high-fat, protein-rich foods, like meats, cheeses, and oils, with grains, bread, and cereals. Don't go overboard with fruit or vegetables or very high-fiber foods as they could cause bowel problems. Stick with familiar, safe foods.

If you have to travel to the race do your best to stay on your usual eating schedule. You may want to bring along some of your favorite nonperishable foods. Call ahead to find out about some of the restaurants and food stores around your hotel. And try to stay at a hotel with a kitchen that can accommodate your needs.

As far as fluids go, use the days before the race to superhydrate. Avoid alcohol and cut back on caffeine, and drink so that your urine is consistently clear and frequent.

The night before the race eat a high-carbohydrate meal containing 800 to 1,000 calories. Again, stick with tried and true foods, drink lots of water, and get plenty of rest.

Race Day

The morning of the race eat a light breakfast, two to four hours before starting time, consisting mainly of high-carbohydrate, low-fiber, low-glycemic foods like oatmeal, or other whole grain cereals, rice, or pasta. If you can't bring yourself to eat in the morning hours before the race—and some of us can't—try a liquid meal, which may be better tolerated, or eat some rice or pasta before bed the night before.

During the race itself follow the patterns that you have practiced during training. Drink ½–¾ cup of fluid every fifteen to twenty minutes throughout the run and ingest 40–70 grams of carbohydrates every hour, as tolerated. Have a distinct, well-practiced plan of what and how much you will eat and drink. If possible, station friends or family at different points on the course to hand you drinks or snacks. Be careful not consume just anything that onlookers are passing out. Water is a safe bet, but other beverages or food could disagree with you and make for an uncomfortable experience.

You Did It!

Postrace refueling is key to a fast recovery. So follow the principles you learned during training. Drink plenty of fluids, two cups for every pound you shed, and eat carbohydrate-rich foods as soon as you can tolerate them. Try liquids first and then move on to solid foods when your appetite allows. During the twenty-four hour period following the race, you'll consume 2,400 to 2,600 calories' worth of carbohydrates to restore your muscle glycogen completely.

It may not be a very good replacement drink, but beer is a good celebration drink, and it's a favorite of many runners. So once you've rehydrated and carbed up feel free to sit back and have a brew or a piece of cheesecake, if that's your passion. Indulge yourself. You've earned it.

Take It with You

The diet that fuels a successful marathon is the same one that fuels success in everyday life. You will need fewer calories as you return to more moderate activity levels, but the basic principles of good eating are constant. So hang on to the habits you develop during training, and always remember the energized feeling of being well nourished.

BREAKFAST

1½ oz cereal
1 cup low-fat milk
½ cup strawberries
1 slice of toast, lightly buttered

MIDMORNING SNACK

1 cup low-fat yogurt
1 banana

LUNCH

Turkey (4 oz) sandwich
Green salad with Italian dressing
Cup of vegetable soup

DURING RUN

2 cups sports drink or a banana

POSTRUN SNACK

2 oz pretzels
1½ cups juice

DINNER

1½ cups pasta with tomato sauce
3 oz chicken breast
2 oz Parmesan cheese
1 cup sautéed broccoli

EVENING SNACK

1 apple
2 oatmeal cookies

8

Running the Race of Your Life

There's an old saying: Be careful what you wish for, because you might get it.

All through the winter of 1995, as I trained for the Los Angeles marathon, I kept wishing, "Please, don't let it be 90 degrees on race day. I won't be acclimated to the heat, and I'll die out there. Please don't let it be 90 degrees."

It wasn't.

On March 4, 1995, the morning of the tenth City of Los Angeles Marathon, the rain came down in torrents. And as I stood with nineteen thousand other runners on the start line near the Los Angeles Coliseum, watching it rain harder as we waited for honorary race chairman Muhammad Ali to fire the starting gun, I was reminded of that old saying—and an essential truth about marathon running.

You can't prepare for everything. At some point, you have to recognize that there are things beyond your control, such as the weather. What you *do* have control over is yourself. How you approach the final days leading up to the race, mentally and physically, is nearly as important as your long runs. So let's look at these final steps, as you get ready to run the race of your life.

PRERACE

You've done your last long run—you've got three weeks left until the big day. The tendency for most beginners at this point is to want to do more. To fine-tune. To get in yet another long run.

Resist this urge.

"You can't cram for the final," says Gordon Bakoulis. "By that, I mean you're not going to get any fitter during the last couple of weeks before the race. So don't try cramming in any last-minute long runs or extra training. The best thing you can do for your body is rest."

As we noted earlier, you may want to think about jumping into a local road race—a 5K or 10K—two weeks before the race, if only to get your legs moving, to practice taking water, to be part of the race ambiance.

The weekend before the marathon, go out for an easy 10-miler. The purpose here is not to get any fitter, but simply to get yourself into the race-day "groove." Practice your form, feel your relaxed strides. Imagine yourself in the marathon, running the same way: easily, effortlessly.

This is a form of visualization—a technique used by sports psychologists. But New York Road Runners Club coach Bob Glover believes that every runner can and should practice visualization, which he describes as "running a movie of the race in your mind's eye." In this mental movie, you can actually see yourself getting up on the morning of the race, having your clothes ready with your numbers pinned on, getting into your car or onto the bus on time, and riding to the start. You see yourself at a certain pace, taking water at each mile, and so on. The whole idea, Glover explains, is that by visualizing these things, you won't be surprised on race day, and you'll minimize the chances of something happening that will throw you off. "It doesn't have to be an exact science," he says. "But it really builds confidence."

That's something we could all use a little of before a marathon. Another way to bolster your confidence is to simply look back and see how far you've come. Peruse your training log. Think back to the point when the idea of running ten miles, much less twenty, seemed ridiculous. The day before my first marathon, the Marine Corps Marathon, I ran into Jeff Galloway when I was picking up my race number. I didn't know him then, and I eagerly told him, in great detail, about every one of the long runs I'd done before the race. He listened patiently and nodded. "It's in the bank," he said. "It's in the bank."

I knew what he meant: if you've made the deposits, you can cash the check. On race day, you're going to draw on every bit of your resources. If you've done the proper training, then you've got sufficient resources to cover that check. If not, be honest with yourself. If, for some reason, you haven't been able to get in the proper training, there's no shame in waiting until you are ready. Remember, there's always another marathon. But there's only one way to run any marathon: that's to be prepared.

Of course, preparation extends through the morning of the race. Whenever I'm part of any premarathon panels, one of the most common questions I hear is, "What should I do leading up to the race?"

Well, we've already told you a few things: relax, rest, visualize. But the short answer to that question is:

Do whatever you've been doing.

The week before the race is not the time to change your training or diet. Take care of all the little details ahead of time—from working out what you'll wear and how you'll get to and from the race, to pinning your number on and deciding what to eat on race morning.

Those details may seem mundane, but they are worthy of your attention. In the 1987 New York City Marathon, I ran with a colleague from my newspaper, Al Cohn. He wore a shirt that said MY NAME IS AL. I wore a generic Nike singlet. For thirteen miles, all I heard from the crowd was, "Way to go, Al!," "Looking good, Al," "You can do it, Al."

Finally, I mumbled something about feeling like a second banana. Al looked at me. "Well, what do you expect them to say to you? 'Go Nike'?"

He was right. Although we both finished the race, I was certainly more anonymous—until the last couple of miles. There, amidst eight trillion spectators in Central Park, I spotted my buddy Paul—a friend from New Hampshire who just happened to be in New York that weekend and had told me he'd "try and look for me." Fat chance, I thought. But when I saw him, late in the race, I literally jumped for joy.

It gave me an adrenaline boost that I needed to finish that race.

Why am I telling you this as part of the prerace preparation? Because in addition to getting a personalized, or at least distinctive, singlet (which you should run with a couple of times before the marathon to make sure it's comfortable), one of the other details you might want to tend to is inviting friends and family to come watch you. In New York, this marathon viewing is a sort of science: the newspapers publish maps showing how you can view the race from several different vantage points along the course, using the subways. Depending on which marathon you're running, it may not need to be that complicated. But however you work it out, your own little rooting section never hurts— nor does the thought of friends and loved ones waiting for you, cheering for you at the finish line.

Back to the prerace prep. There is a lot of discussion about how to "taper." Over the years, the running magazines have published very specific and complex regimens on just what to do on each day leading up to race morning. The purpose of this book is to simplify and to provide you with the basics. And the basic truth of tapering, as we've said, is to follow your exercise and eating regimen as you have— with a couple of caveats.

Try to get a couple of days of complete rest before the race. The day before the race, you may want to stretch your legs, probably by walking a little bit. But if you really feel antsy, there's nothing wrong with doing a very, very easy jog for a mile or two. "It can have a calming effect," says Amby Burfoot. "Just don't get carried away. And don't spend all day on your feet, walking around the expo or sightseeing."

Instead, make sure you've taken care of all the little things; the details that will help you stay relaxed and minimize problems on race day. To help you, here's a little prerace checklist:

❦ Get a good night's sleep two nights before the race. Research shows this is when it will benefit you most. Don't forget to set a back-up alarm clock or get a wake-up call from your hotel.

❦ Make sure you know how you're getting to the start line and how you're getting home from the finish. Many races offer shuttle buses to and from local hotels or other central locations; if you're in doubt, call the race office or your hotel.

❦ Plan on what you're going to wear based on current weather conditions. Don't overdress: you don't want to be overheated later in the race. To keep yourself comfortable while you're waiting around for the start, plan to bring an old long-sleeve T-shirt or sweatshirt that you can discard after the race starts.

❦ Pin your number to your race shirt the night before. Why start marathon morning by drawing blood . . . especially your own?

❦ Pack a bag that will be waiting for you at the baggage-check area at the finish, or with whomever is going to meet you. Make sure you include a bottle of water, some emergency money, and a change of clothes for after the race, including sweatshirt and pants, in case it's cold.

❦ Don't vary your diet. There's no need to surprise your stomach the day before the race. Stick with what you know works best for you.

❦ Don't go overboard at the race pasta party. The prerace pasta party has become a ritual for marathoners. Go ahead and enjoy, but whatever you eat in the evening before, don't overeat. Instead, consider eating a large carbohydrate-rich lunch, allowing you more time to digest. And save the alcohol until after the race.

❦ Clip your toenails.

❦ Drink plenty of fluids.

❦ Don't worry about the weather. Just try to prepare for it. If it's going to rain, bring a hat; if it's going to be cold, a pair of lightweight gloves or mittens.

❦ Relax as best you can. Practice the visualization techniques Glover recommends, read a good book, watch a diverting movie on TV. The less tense you are going into the race, the better you'll run.

RACE MORNING

Your first assignment for marathon morning: try to eat something. "One of the biggest food mistakes made by marathoners is eating too little beforehand," notes sports nutritionist Nancy Clark. "They fear that food will result in an upset stomach. Be sure to eat premarathon foods that are tried and true. Some runners can eat a bagel, juice, or a light breakfast one to three hours before a marathon; many carry familiar foods with them to the start."

If you're making a face while you read this, I sympathize. It's hard for me to eat first thing in the morning on race day, too. But again, my own experience may be helpful here: in 1988, I ran the now defunct Stamford (Connecticut) Marathon, which began at noon. I had time to eat a full breakfast that morning—and I never felt as good during or after a marathon as I did that year. I was actually able to "kick" the last couple of miles, something I've never done before or since.

Most of the other marathons I've done, including Los Angeles, started too early for me to eat. That's a mistake. I should have risen a half hour earlier and eaten something.

In addition to eating you should, of course, continue to take fluids. Bring a bottle of water along to the start, and sip it while you wait—just in case you can't get any in the confusion before the race. Also, apply vaseline. Some runners go wild with this, turning themselves into virtual reservoirs of petroleum jelly. Apply some at least to the sensitive spots—especially the crotch, nipples, and around the toes.

Another thing you should consider on marathon morning is a warm-up. Yes, I know it sounds strange to warm up when you're going to be running for hours, but when the gun goes off, you'll feel better if the muscles are warm and your fuel pump is "primed."

"A warm-up prepares your body for the intensive activity to come," says exercise physiologist Ann Marie Miller of New York Sports Clubs. "It's like starting a car motor," says Miller. "You wouldn't go out in the dead of winter, put a key in your most expensive Lexis, and then burn rubber out of the driveway. You'd let it idle for a while, and then begin driving, and gradually pick up speed. It's the same thing with your body. A proper warm-up helps to gradually start up the physical mechanisms and the metabolic processes that are important for any sport."

A proper warm-up can consist of simply performing the same activity—whether it's walking or stationary biking or running—but at a lesser intensity: for example, Miller's marathon warm-ups consist primarily of some brisk walking and jogging in place, plus some gentle stretches. The idea is to gradually raise the body temperature, promote blood flow to the working muscles, and by mimicking the running movement to provide a "rehearsal affect" for the runners.

Ultramarathon champion Stu Mittleman, urges caution: "I would say when participating in any warm-up, especially one before the marathon, do not attempt to do any stretching or movement that you haven't done on a regular basis," he says. "If they're jogging in place, doing breathing exercises, fine. But I think the most important thing for people to do before the race is to hydrate, relax, and get to the starting line as calmly as possible."

Mittleman believes that the ideal marathon warm-up would be to have the entire field walk briskly together for a half-mile to the starting line. Doing some kind of low-intensity movement prior to the race is important for another reason: it can help stimulate the body's fat burning mechanisms, thereby sparing glycogen—the carbohydrate-based fuel that is stored in the muscles.

Some interesting research was done on this in the 1980s by a team of exercise physiologists at Southern Illinois University. The results of their study suggested that marathoners who warm up by walking before the race will start burning fat earlier and more efficiently than those who don't. "Typically, when you start exercising without warming up, you burn more carbohydrates than fat," said Ronald Hetzler, the principal author of the study. By warming up properly before a prolonged endurance event like the marathon, the researchers found, you'll burn more fat and proportionately fewer carbohydrates throughout the duration of your run. That's critical. You don't want your carbohydrate meter running on empty. "Hitting the wall" is a depletion of glycogen, the carbohydrate-based fuel that is stored in the muscles.

Some brisk walking before a marathon, Hetzler and his colleagues found, will help conserve those carbs. The researchers calculated that runners who walked before the forty-minute run used for the test burned 15 more grams of fat and 23 fewer grams of carbohydrates than the runners who didn't warm up. Those 23 grams represent the equivalent of enough energy for about another 1.5 miles of running! "Our suggestion is that marathoners should not use the first few miles of a race as a warm-up," said Hetzler. Instead, he recommends walking at a brisk pace for twenty minutes before the start of the race. That will get your body burning fat and sparing the carbohydrates for when you really need them—the last few miles.

You don't have to make this warm-up into a regimen or a race. Indeed, you may have to walk simply to get over to the starting area from your hotel or the parking lot. Just make sure you start moving a little bit before the race.

THE RACE

Four words about your race strategy: Start slow. Finish strong.

"The marathon is a race of attrition," says 2:16 marathoner Mike Keohane, assistant cross-country coach at Columbia University. "There are very, very few marathoners—even among the top level—who can go out fast and hold it for the entire race. Try to exercise self-control. That's how you run a good marathon: by running the first half slower than the second."

For beginners, that means keeping your head. There's nothing more absurd than back-of-the-pack hot dogs who go bolting off at the start in order to lead the race momentarily and perhaps get their faces on TV. Pay no attention to those who go charging past you for the first couple of miles. Run within yourself. Even the elite runners allow others to get ahead of them at that point—they know the real race doesn't begin until much, much later.

A key question here for followers of the Galloway program is whether to take regular walking breaks during the marathon as you have during your long training runs. Galloway believes that you should continue a pattern of five minutes of running followed by one minute of walking throughout the race. Some people aren't comfortable with that: they feel that if they haven't run every step of the race, they've somehow shortchanged themselves.

You're going to have to be your own judge here. You've probably done some walking during your long runs. But you may have found that you were able to complete those runs with little or no walking breaks. Whatever you do, race day is not the time to experiment—certainly not in the first half of the race. If you feel strong the second half, run the entire way. If not, maintain those walking intervals: you'll be surprised to see how many others are walking by that point . . . and most of them didn't plan it that way!

I'll say it again: run conservatively. The first ten miles of the race should feel almost effortless. If it doesn't, slow down! Remember: you're in this to finish and feel good.

That good feeling will be facilitated by taking water early and often. Because it takes up to twenty minutes for water to be absorbed by the body, you shouldn't wait until you're thirsty. It may be too late then. Most experts recommend that you take water at every opportunity early in the race. If the weather's hot, take two cups—you can pour one on your head to cool yourself off if necessary (although, remember: you'll receive the greatest benefits from the water you drink).

Also, be careful what you take: many marathons have sports drinks and water set up on separate tables. If you're not paying attention you may make a sticky mistake: New York City-based coach Tracy Sundlun tells the story of one his runners who mixed up her cups: she drank the water and threw the Gatorade over her head.

Some people, somewhat sheepishly, have told me that they were afraid to take water because they were afraid of having to go to the bathroom. Not to worry: if you have to relieve yourself, so be it. There are portable toilets along the courses of most marathons (check the race application, or ask a race volunteer before the start, if you're unsure).

Between water stops, try to get into a rhythm—and take a page out of the ultramarathoner's book. Most of these runners, who participate in 50-, 100-mile, and 24-hour events, break their races down into segments: 10 miles, half marathon, 20 miles. Try to do the same thing here. At mile 4, you don't want to be thinking "only 22.2 to go!" You want to be focusing on hitting 5—and feeling good and staying on pace. Get into a rhythm with your stride, feel loose.

Ask most marathoners to recall their first race and you get a furrowed brow, a quizzical look, maybe one vivid detail: Rae Baymiller remembers the sound of thousands of feet hitting the pavement; Chris Shihadeh remembers the crowd, "reaching out, cheering as if you're doing something fantastic." Gloria Averbuch remembers thinking she hadn't realized anything could be that hard—and at the end, wanting to do it all over again.

So enjoy the sights and sounds around you—but don't let the crowds or the weather or the other runners around you throw you off your game plan. There's a natural tendency to pick up the pace when people are applauding you. You can nod, wave, and look as heroic as you want—but don't start running faster. You'll pay for it later.

If you're well trained and you run intelligently (read: conservatively), the miles will begin to roll by. Five, 10, half marathon, 15. Remember those long training runs on beautiful mornings with your friends. You should still feel good at this point; if not, slow down a little. Walk if necessary.

At 20 miles, some people begin to freak out. This is when runners supposedly "hit the wall." This wall—which we mentioned earlier—is often talked about but rarely encountered, except by people who haven't eaten properly or done their homework. "If you've done those long runs, you don't need to be afraid of it," said Baymiller.

Still, 20 is a significant milestone. Competitors will tell you that this last 10K is where the marathon really begins, where the race is won or lost.

You're not running to win anything. Still, I'll be honest: it's not going to be easy. You're going to have to dig deep. "I often use relaxation tips at this point," says Grete Waitz. "I tell myself to relax each part of the body: neck, shoulders, arms. Then I repeat some words like 'steady, push' to keep up the pace and confidence."

Sometimes that confidence erodes very quickly. And it may even happen before the 20-mile mark. What happens when the mind says no? Sometimes, things you wouldn't believe. The story of my friend Bill Foster, running his first marathon in New York, is instructive.

Bill made a typical rookie mistake. He went out too fast.

A little past the halfway point, he dropped out. "I felt shot," he said. "I stepped off the course and thought 'Well, that's it.' I worked my way through the crowd and sat down on a stoop. Across the street was a pizzeria, and I thought, 'Okay, I'll get some pizza and figure out how to get home.' I was out . . . I was done. But then, this woman came up to me and she said, 'You know, tomorrow they won't ask you about time, they'll ask you whether you finished. If you walk, you can still finish.' I said, 'You've got a point there.' So I walked into a supermarket next to the pizzeria, and with a couple of dollars I had stuck into my shoe, I bought two candy bars and ate them. I started to walk, and eventually I was able to jog again. I finished the race, running, and was able to tell that to everybody in the office and at home. The worst thing was that I never got to thank that woman."

The lessons? First, as we've said, don't worry about your time, and don't go out too fast. Second, spectators can play an important role in the event. But finally, and most important, don't underestimate yourself. Remember: sometimes the body is willing, but the mind isn't. If you change your mind, you can change the outcome of your race.

THE FINISH

The outcome of my marathon wasn't looking too promising. By mile 22, I was hurting. The rain was pouring down on Los Angeles, and although I wasn't ready to quit (how could I justify flying across the country if I did?), I wasn't happy. Fortunately, I had a friend, too—and unlike the unknown Good Samarathon who helped Bill Foster, mine was somebody I knew—an old high school friend, Larry Indiviglia, who lives in San Diego and had come up to L.A. to run the second half of the race with me. I was sure glad he did. "Just keep moving," he told me. "One foot in front of the other. One mile at a time."

That kept me going for a couple of miles. Then I started to crave Gatorade. (Marathon running, I think, has at least one thing in common with pregnancy—I often hear stories about runners developing cravings late in the race; and sometimes for things a lot stranger than a sports drink!) The mental picture of that cup of Gatorade kept me going between miles 23 and 24. But at the 24-mile water stop . . . Ouch! No Gatorade. In retrospect, maybe it was better that way. Between the craving and Larry's exhortations, it got me one mile further. There, I got my Gatorade. A couple of sips and a whole lot of adrenaline that began to surge as I could hear the crowds at the finish line got me to the end.

The finish line of every marathon is an emotional scene. But, for me, Los Angeles was especially moving. Maybe it was because with the rain and fierce winds in our faces, L.A. was about the toughest marathon I've ever done—and therefore the most satisfying to finish. You'll see what I mean, as you approach the finish area. The last quarter mile is remarkable: the crowds are densely packed, they're all yelling and cheering, maybe there are even some faces you know. A few more strides and you've done it. It's automatic now—this is what you've been teaching your body to do, for months. You cross the line. Smile for the cameras, raise a fist, high-five the person behind you, if you've got the energy.

Congratulations. You wished you could do a marathon . . . and you did.

Beyond the Marathon

When you cross the finish line of your first marathon, your first inclination will be to stop immediately.

Don't do it: to minimize the soreness in your legs over the days to come, you need to keep walking. Some of this you'll have to do—you'll have to walk through the finish line chutes to get into the family reunion area. But don't stop there: even as you meet and greet, keep moving.

Galloway recommends walking a mile immediately after the race and, later on, 2 to 3 miles more to help "flush out" the lactic acid—the waste product of exercise—that causes the soreness in your muscles.

What else should you do directly after the race? Savor the moment . . . and sip on a sports drink to quickly replace some of those carbs.

Then, take care of your body.

A massage can work wonders after a marathon—which is why, in most races, you'll see a long line outside the massage tents in the finish line area (these are often provided free: check your race application and instructions to find out if this service will be offered at your marathon). If you're staying at a hotel with a pool and a health club, take advantage of it: an easy swim or a sit-down in the whirlpool will help. At the very least, slip into a nice hot bath to soothe the muscles and do some gentle stretching.

Take proper care after the race, and you won't be one of those people telling postmarathon horror stories about barely being able to climb stairs for a few days. Some soreness is expected and normal, but if you treat your body well the night of the marathon, you'll be full of spunk the next morning and ready to brag about your achievements.

Don't forget to celebrate: as we said in chapter 7, the night after your first marathon is not the time to be watching your diet. You've earned your reward—take it, whether it's in the form of a beer or two or a slice of cheesecake. But as far as running, I wouldn't even think about it for at least a week; and even then, it should be very easy jogging. You've asked a lot from your body—now give it a rest from running.

You'll probably still want to do something, and in the days after the marathon, some form of "active" rest can help in your recovery, physically and mentally. Thom Birch, a marathon runner and yoga teacher in New York, recalls the advice offered by his old coach, Al Lawrence, a former

Olympic marathoner from Australia. "He used to have his runners walk six miles straight for three days straight after the marathon," recalls Birch. "It gets the blood going and there's no pounding. I recommend that you do something similar, some form of 'active recovery' outside of what you usually do: walking, yoga, swimming, cycling. Also, a lot of people are mentally exhausted after the marathon. Maybe it's time for some meditation, or way to divert your interests: a symphony, a good book, a vacation."

Good advice: you don't necessarily have to walk six miles, but walking (or cycling or swimming) even for thirty to forty minutes each day after the marathon will help you. While you're recovering, it might also help you to spend a couple of more hours a day with the important people of your life. Chances are, they've had to play second fiddle to your training program for the last few months.

Relish the feeling of having finished your first marathon—you can even go over the race to see what you might do differently next time around—but don't start planning your next race right away. Even the very best runners rarely do more than two or three a year. *One* marathon a year is probably a reasonable and safe goal for the average runner. If you've followed Galloway's conservative program faithfully, you should have survived this race without any serious injuries or physical problems. That's great. That's the best you can feel. But don't tempt fate by trying another one any time too soon.

We can learn a lesson from some of those who got caught up in the Running Boom of the 1970s and early 1980s. "We used to run several marathons a year . . . sometimes, two in six months," recalls Bud Rourke, a Massapequa, Long Island, resident who started running seriously at that time. "The concept of cross-training didn't even exist in our minds. Stretching was putting your leg up on a log and touching your toes a couple of times before you started. We just ran, ran, ran, ran."

Eventually, he ran into trouble: After twelve marathons in seven years, Bud got hurt. And hurt again . . . and again. By 1993, Bud had a medical sheet that looked like a pro football player's: he'd had Achilles tendon surgery, two knee surgeries, and a serious back injury.

The good news is that Bud is back. But now, he says, he trains more intelligently. He stretches twenty minutes a day, lifts weights, uses a cross-country ski machine, and runs. He'll probably never run a marathon again (he says half marathons are long enough for him, thank you). Still, he'll never forget the feeling of finishing his first marathon. "It was euphoric," he says. "But for me, it didn't wear off. We just kept going and going and did it again." If you're feeling that same glow, enjoy it, but don't get carried away by it. "Don't get greedy," Bud says. "Get smart. Give your body a chance to heal. If you're going to run another marathon, don't rush into it."

Of course, you may choose *never* to run another marathon. But I suspect you will still want to be challenged athletically—perhaps in another endurance sport, such as the triathlon, or maybe in shorter-distance road races, or even distances over 31 miles (50K)—the *ultra*marathons.

For me, one of the most interesting outcomes from the Los Angeles marathon was that I went on, at age forty, to run some of the fastest times of my life on the roads, including a sub-five-minute mile that September. I thought it was remarkable, but one of my training partners, Patty DiFalco, made a good observation: the long runs and the marathon early in the year, she said, had provided an aerobic foundation—a base—that I could build on in order to do faster work that summer and fall.

Still, I know the time will come again when I'll get the itch to do another marathon. If you get that marathon bug too, you may keep itching for years to come—and it will probably be for different reasons than it was the first time. Consider the results of this study, reported in the October 1995 issue of *Running & FitNews*, in which five hundred male and female marathoners were asked about their motivations:

❦ Those who ran their first marathons did so for health, weight control, and a sense of self-esteem and achievement of personal goals.

❦ Runners with two or three marathons under their belts were more concerned with improving their performances.

❦ Veterans with more than three marathons completed had incorporated marathon running into their personal and social identity and looked for recognition from others for their marathon running. In other words, marathon running had become a part of their lifestyle.

You may follow the same sort of progression. Much of this book urges you to downplay your finish time in your debut marathon. Now that you know you can go the distance, you may want to start thinking about doing it within a certain time. That will require more intense training and certainly more total miles than you did under the beginner's program outlined here. If that's a goal, I recommend looking into some of the books for competitive marathoners written by coaches such as Gordon Bakoulis, Bob Glover and, yes, Jeff Galloway (see "For More Information" in Appendix II).

There is so much to learn about this event: I ran my personal best time in my seventh marathon. I've heard of some runners who did it in their thirtieth or fourtieth attempt at the distance! Whether they run faster or slower, everyone seems to get something out of it. "Every time I run a marathon, I learn something new about the race and about myself," Grete Waitz says. That is one of the great rewards of running marathons, whether you do just one or fifty. Wherever your road takes you, I hope you'll carry the lessons and the memories you learned from *your* marathon through the rest of your life.

Appendix I

Training Schedule

Logging the Miles

Jeff Galloway's 16-week training program for first-time marathoners starts at the 6-mile mark; that is, your first long run (alternative three to five minutes running and one minute walking) in your first week should be 6 miles in length. If you're not up to that long a "run/walk," simply start at a lesser distance and figure in a few more weeks of training time.

The schedule for the Monday-through-Saturday workouts is the same each week; Sunday's long run adds to the fun. To keep things even livelier and to put less wear and tear on your joints, consider cross-training, using a few different low-impact sports: swimming, bicycling, in-line skating, and low-impact aerobics are good options.

Stretch the schedule out as long as you'd like, but don't shorten it. As Gordon Bakoulis says, "There is never any need to rush into doing a marathon." Treat your body well by giving it ample training, rest, nutrition, and hydration, and it will repay you—in marathon kind.

Week 1:

Monday:	Rest
Tuesday:	Weights or cross-training
Wednesday:	Run thirty minutes*
Thursday:	Weights or cross-training
Friday:	Run thirty minutes*
Saturday:	Walk or cross-training
Sunday:	Long run, 6 miles

Weekly Long Runs:

Week	Miles	Week	Miles
2	8	10	8
3	10	11	20 to 22
4	6	12	8 to 10
5	12 to 13	13	8 to 10
6	6	14	22 to 24
7	15 to 16	15	8 to 10
8	7	16	8 to 10
9	18 to 19	17	Marathon

*When you're well into the program and you feel like going longer than thirty minutes, make sure you keep these runs to no longer than 4 to 6 miles.

Appendix II

For More Information:

Books

Block, Gordon Bakoulis. *How to Train For and Run Your Best Marathon.* New York, Fireside, 1993.

Clark, Nancy, and Gloria Averbuch. *The New York City Marathon Cookbook.* Nashville: Rutledge Hill Press, 1994.

Derderian, Tom. *Boston Marathon: The History of the World's Premier Running Event*. Champaign, IL: Human Kinetics, 1994.

Ellis, Joe, and Joe Henderson. *Running Injury-Free*. Emmaus, PA: Rodale Press, 1994.

Galloway, Jeff. *Galloway's Book on Running*. Bolinas, CA: Shelter Publications, 1984.

Gambaccini, Peter. *The New York City Marathon: 25 Years*. New York: Rizzoli, 1994.

Glover, Bob, and Pete Schuder. *The New Competitive Runners Handbook*. 2nd ed. New York: Penguin Books, 1988.

Hanc, John. *The Essential Runner: A Concise Guide to the Basics for All Runners*. New York: Lyons & Burford, 1994.

Samuelson, Joan, and Gloria Averbuch. *Joan Samuelson's Running for Women*. Emmaus, PA: Rodale Press, 1994.

Treadwell, Sandy. *The World of Marathons*. New York: Stewart, Tabori and Chang, 1987.

MAGAZINES

Runner's World
For subscription information, write P.O. Box 7307, Red Oak, IA 51591-0307 or call (800) 666-2828.

Running Times
For subscription information, write P.O. Box 50016, Boulder, CO 80322-0016 or call (800) 816-4735.

American Runner
For subscription information, write 137 Clinton Avenue, New Rochelle, NY 10801 or call (914) 576-0971.

Newsletters

Running & FitNews
American Running and Fitness Association
4405 East/West Highway, Suite 405
Bethesda, MD 20814
(800) 776-ARFA

Running Research News
P.O. Box 27041
Lansing, MI 48909
(517) 371-4447

Other Sources of Information on Marathons and Training

Road Runners Club of America
629 South Washington Street, Suite 250
Alexandria, VA 22314
(703) 836-0558

New York Road Runners Club
9 East 89th Street
New York, NY 10128
(212) 860-4455

Jeff Galloway's Marathon Program
P.O. Box 76843
Atlanta, GA 30358
(404) 255-1033

Top 10
United States
Marathons

Here are the ten largest U.S. marathons (based on 1994 finishers). Each entry includes the month the race is held and the address and phone number for more information.

HONOLULU (27,008)
Honolulu, HI/December
Honolulu Marathon
   Association
3435 Wailae Avenue, #208
Honolulu, HI 96816
(808) 734-7200

NEW YORK CITY (26,754)
New York, NY/ November
New York Road Runners Club
9 East 89th Street
New York, NY 10128
(212) 860-4455

CITY OF LOS ANGELES
   (15,186)
Los Angeles, CA/March
11110 West Ohio Avenue,
   Suite 100
Los Angeles, CA 90025
(310) 444-5544

MARINE CORPS (14,618)
Washington, DC/October
   or November
P.O. Box 188
Quantico, VA 22134
(703) 640-2225

CHICAGO MARATHON
   (8,641)
Chicago, IL/October
101 West Grand Avenue
Chicago, IL 60610
(312) 527-2200

BOSTON (8,258)
Boston, MA/April
Boston Athletic Association
P.O. Box 1995
Hopkinton, MA 01748
(508) 435-6905

WALT DISNEY WORLD
(5,816)
Orlando, FL/January
P.O. Box 10,000
Lake Vista, FL 32830
(407) 939-7810

TWIN CITIES (5,693)
St. Paul, MN/October
708 North First Street,
    Suite CR-33
Minneapolis, MN 55401
(612) 673-0778

GRANDMA'S (5,258)
Duluth, MN/June
P.O. Box 16234
Duluth, MN 55816
(218) 727-0947

PORTLAND (5,070)
Portland, OR/October
Les Smith
P.O. Box 4040
Beaverton, OR 97076
(503) 226-1111

SOURCES: USA Track & Field Road Running Information Center
Runner's World

INDEX